NOAH HAIDLE
THREE PLAYS

Noah Haidle is a graduate of Princeton University and The Juilliard School, where he was a Lila Acheson Wallace playwright-in-residence. He is the recipient of three Lincoln Center Le Compte Du Nuoy Awards, the 2005 Helen Merrill Award for Emerging Playwrights and an NEA/TCG Residency Program for Playwrights grant. His plays include *Mr Marmalade* (South Coast Repertory, Costa Mesa, CA; Roundabout Theatre Company, New York, NY; Contemporary American Theater Festival, West Virginia; Silo Theater Company, Auckland, New Zealand), *Kitty Kitty Kitty* (Summer Play Festival, New York, NY), *Princess Marjorie* (South Coast Repertory, Costa Mesa, CA), *Rag and Bone* (Long Wharf Theatre, New Haven, CT; Rattlestick Theater, New York, NY), *A Long History of Neglect* (Mildred's Umbrella Theater Company, Houston, TX), *Vigils* (The Goodman Theatre, Chicago, IL; The Woolly Mammoth Theater Company, Washington DC), *Persephone* (The Huntington Theater Company, Boston, MA) and *The Perfect Hours* (The Juilliard School, New York, NY).

T0347814

Noah Haidle

THREE PLAYS

RAG AND BONE
MR MARMALADE
VIGILS

OBERON BOOKS
LONDON

First published in 2007 by Oberon Books Ltd
521 Caledonian Road, London N7 9RH
Tel: +44 (0) 20 7607 3637 / Fax: +44 (0) 20 7607 3629
e-mail: info@oberonbooks.com
www.oberonbooks.com

PB ISBN: 9781840027501
E ISBN: 9781783198467

Cover design by Oberon Books

eBook conversion by Lapiz Digital Services, India.

Contents

RAG AND BONE, 7

MR MARMALADE, 85

VIGILS, 153

Contents

RAG AND BONE

for Pepper,
who knew it was hers even before I did

'A mound of refuse or the sweepings of a street,
Old kettles, old bottles, and a broken can,
Old iron, old bones, old rags, that raving slut
Who keeps the till. Now that my ladder's gone
I must lie down where all the ladders start
In the foul rag and bone shop of the heart.'

   – from 'The Circus Animals' Desertion' (1939)
      by William Butler Yeats

Characters

JEFF

GEORGE

HOOKER

POET

T-BONE

CUSTOMER

MILLIONAIRE

WAITER

Rag and Bone was first performed on 2 February 2005 at the Long Wharf Theatre in New Haven, Connecticut, with the following company:

JEFF, Ian Brennan
GEORGE, Justin Hagan
HOOKER, Annie Golden
POET, David Bishins
T-BONE, Frederick Owens
CUSTOMER / WAITER, Carolyn Baeumler
MILLIONAIRE, Tom Riis Farrell

Directed by Tina Landau
Set design by G W Mercier
Costume design by Candice Donnelly
Lighting design by Scott Zielinkski
Sound design by John Gromada
Dramaturg Beatrice Basso
Production Stage Manager Lori Lundquist

Act One

1

The Ladder Store.
There are ladders everywhere.
JEFF tends the store. Checks on some ladders.
In comes GEORGE wearing a ski mask. He's got an igloo cooler with
him.

JEFF: Hey.

GEORGE: Hey.

JEFF: I was thinking, do you think you could build a ladder
    that goes all the way to the moon?

GEORGE: No. That's impossible.

JEFF: Why?

GEORGE: The ozone layer, the earth's rotation, insurance.

JEFF: What about a ladder to heaven?

GEORGE: Heaven doesn't exist.

JEFF: That's where Mom is.

    She said she'd wait for me.

GEORGE: Mom is dead in the ground, Jeff.

    She's not waiting for you anywhere.

    (*He takes off his ski mask.*)

JEFF: Don't get jealous. She's waiting for you, too.

    Just before she died she squeezed my hand and said,
    (*Imitating Mom.*) 'I'll wait for you and your brother in
    heaven.'

    What's in the cooler? Is it lunch?

GEORGE: No. It's not lunch.

JEFF: That's too bad. I could really use a sandwich.

    (*GEORGE takes a human heart out of the cooler.*)

    What's that? It looks like a human heart.

GEORGE: These are what I sell to make extra money.

    Remember? It's a widget.

JEFF: I forgot. Widgets look so much like hearts.

GEORGE: This is a very special widget, Jeff. After I unload this widget we're gonna sell the ladder store and move to Bermuda.

JEFF: Sell the ladder store?

GEORGE: Bermuda's right on the ocean. We can go swimming.

JEFF: I can't swim.

GEORGE: You can learn. I'm tired of selling ladders, Jeff.

JEFF: That's because you're not very good at it.

I don't want to tell you how to do your job but when I'm with a customer it's like we're the only two people in the whole universe and I'm completely attune to their wants and needs. And besides. We provide a very important service to the community.

If it weren't for us, how would people get cats out of trees? Or footballs off garages?

GEORGE: I guess I never thought of it like that.

JEFF: I think maybe what you need is a hug.

GEORGE: I don't need a hug.

JEFF: Then maybe I need one.

GEORGE: Do you?

JEFF: Yes, please.

GEORGE: Okay, but just a little one.

JEFF: Just a teensy-weensy hug.

(*GEORGE hugs JEFF. JEFF hugs back. Hard.*)

GEORGE: You lied. This is not a teensy-weensy hug.

JEFF: I exaggerated.

(*GEORGE has to break away.*)

GEORGE: I'm tired, Jeff.

JEFF: So take a nap.

I can handle the store, bro.

GEORGE: I mean, I'm tired of this.

JEFF: You mean the grind?

GEORGE: The store, the widgets, taking care of your
  dumbass –

  I didn't mean that. My tongue got away from me.

JEFF: Don't worry about it.

  My tongue gets away from me all the time.

  It's hard sometimes to even keep it in my mouth.

GEORGE: Maybe I will take that nap.

JEFF: I'll be here.

GEORGE: Okay. See ya later.

JEFF: See ya later.

  (*GEORGE exits.*

  JEFF tends to some ladders.)

2

On the street.
The HOOKER stands on a corner.
The POET stumbles on. He's got a huge bandage over his chest.

HOOKER: Hey, mister, you looking for a party?

POET: A party? No thank you. I wouldn't have fun at a party.

  (*He begins to stumble off.*)

HOOKER: Is it because you got a boo boo? You like bandages,
  honey?

  Come back over here and I'll bandage you all over.

POET: My heart was stolen from me.

  I used to be a poet but I can't feel anything anymore.

HOOKER: You don't have a heart?

POET: No. Just a gaping void.

HOOKER: Let me see.

  (*She peeks under the bandage.*)

  I could make some money with a hole that big.

  Come inside. Let me warm you up.

  (*Knocks on the door. T-BONE opens it. He's a big pimp.*)

T-Bone, let me in, baby. This guy's walking around without a heart. He used to be a poet.

T-BONE: No poets.

HOOKER: Come on, baby.

POET: Is it your birthday, T-Bone?

T-BONE: Is it my what?

POET: Your birthday? I'm sorry. But your friend asked if I was looking for a party. I assumed she was talking about something sexual, but then I thought maybe she was talking about your birthday party.

HOOKER: He didn't mean nothing by that, T-Bone.

T-BONE: My Momma died giving birth to me, so every year on my birthday I have to remember the sacrifice she made. Nobody talks about my birthday, you understand?

HOOKER: How could he have known, T-Bone?

POET: I'm sorry, T-Bone. I didn't mean any offence.

(*T-BONE hits the POET real hard in the stomach. The POET doubles over in pain.*)

HOOKER: T-Bone!

T-BONE: Shut up, baby.

HOOKER: You shouldn't have hit him, T-Bone.

T-BONE: I said shut your trap.

(*He hits her in the stomach. She doubles over in pain.*
T-Bone goes to the door.)

Get inside, baby.

(*She goes to the door.*)

HOOKER: (*Still doubled over.*) It was nice to meet you.

POET: (*Still doubled over.*) You too.

(*She goes inside.*)

T-BONE: Get out of here, freak.

If I catch you here again I'll break your thumbs.

POET: Please, T-Bone. It's so cold outside.

T-BONE: You think it's warm inside? This whole world is cold once we outta our mamas.

You best get used to it.

(*T-BONE slams the door.*
The POET shivers.)
POET: I can feel the cold.
That's something at least.
(*He stumbles off.*)

3

The Ladder Store.
JEFF tends ladders.
GEORGE enters groggy after his nap.

GEORGE: Hey.
JEFF: Hey.
GEORGE: What are you doing?
JEFF: I was just making a list of all the people I'd say hi to
when I go to heaven.
GEORGE: Who's on your list?
JEFF: Mom's first, of course. And then my best friend from
third grade Brandon whose last name I forgot who got hit
by a car. And then Vince Lombardi, and then Grandma,
and then my high school science teacher Mr Chalmers,
and my cat Sneakers. No, wait.
I'd say hi to Sneakers after Vince Lombardi but before
Grandma. She smelled like pickles. And I hate pickles.
GEORGE: Listen, Jeff.
I think it's time I tell you something.
JEFF: I already know where babies come from.
GEORGE: I'm not going to tell you where babies come from.
JEFF: Because I already know.
GEORGE: I need to tell you something about the widgets.
JEFF: Do you need help selling them?
Because I could sell a picture book to a blind man.
GEORGE: No. Just listen.
JEFF: I am listening.

I'm a very good listener.

In school I always got the highest marks for listening. That and leadership.

Isn't that funny? Because I don't think of myself as a natural born leader.

GEORGE: Listen.

JEFF: I'm listening.

GEORGE: You know the extra job I have?

JEFF: Yeah.

GEORGE: I don't sell widgets.

JEFF: Are you an assassin?

GEORGE: No! I'm not an assassin.

JEFF: Are you a sportscaster for Telemundo?

GEORGE: No. I don't know Spanish.

JEFF: Are you gay?

GEORGE: No. And that's not a job.

JEFF: Okay, I give up.

What are you?

GEORGE: Well.

The thing is…

JEFF: …yeah.

You can tell me anything, bro.

GEORGE: Well –

(*A female CUSTOMER enters.*)

JEFF: – this heart to heart is gonna have to wait.

We got a customer.

Good afternoon, welcome to The Ladder Store.

CUSTOMER: Hello. Gosh, you sure do have a lot of ladders.

JEFF: That's our job, miss. What can I help you with today?

CUSTOMER: I'm looking for a special ladder.

JEFF: Are you trying to get to heaven?

CUSTOMER: No.

I was told to come here for a very special ladder.

JEFF: We've got every ladder made today, and some that were made yesterday. That's our motto.

My motto, actually.

GEORGE: I'll handle this customer, Jeff.

Take a break.

JEFF: I don't need a break.

GEORGE: Take lunch.

JEFF: Lunch!

See you later.

CUSTOMER: Goodbye.

(*JEFF leaves.*)

GEORGE: You say you're looking for a very special ladder.

CUSTOMER: Yes. I hate being on the ground.

(*GEORGE takes out a stethoscope. Listens to her heart.*)

GEORGE: What seems to be the problem?

CUSTOMER: It's like in the movie of my life I'm not the lead.

I don't even have a supporting part.

I'm an extra, a silhouette in the background, out of focus, anonymous.

GEORGE: You've come to the right place.

CUSTOMER: You can make me the lead in the movie of my life?

GEORGE: I'll try my best

CUSTOMER: I don't even need to be the lead. Just a couple of good, meaty scenes would be enough.

(*GEORGE takes out cooler. Holds up hearts, one at a time.*)

GEORGE: Here we have a very nice heart. Took it off a pediatrician who loved children more than anything in the world. She used to give free medical care to anyone in need.

This is a nice heart as well. Took it off a public defender who helped all the neediest cases. And even though the system is corrupt she kept with it.

CUSTOMER: What about that one?

GEORGE: I see you have a very good eye.

This is the heart of a poet.

(*He takes out the heart of the POET, which should look pretty much like all the other hearts.*)

Took it off a poet who lived his whole life in pursuit of truth and beauty.

This heart would let you see the world with a profound clarity. You'd see people as they truly are. And would give you a sense of empathy that borders on the clairvoyant.

You would feel other people's suffering.

CUSTOMER: How much is it?

GEORGE: Please don't take offence to this. But I don't think you could handle the heart of a poet.

CUSTOMER: I used to write poetry.

In college.

GEORGE: Please. Let's move on.

CUSTOMER: Fine.

Tell me more about the public defender.

GEORGE: You'll feel lots and lots of things with this heart. Empathy. Passion. Mercy.

This is a very, very good heart.

CUSTOMER: But it's not the heart of a poet.

GEORGE: No.

CUSTOMER: Will you be getting any minor poets?

Something I could handle.

GEORGE: I can never predict my inventory. I may get one tomorrow. I may not get one for ten years.

CUSTOMER: Tell me about the pediatrician.

GEORGE: Mostly you would feel an enormous sense of compassion. And deserved righteousness.

CUSTOMER: What's that other one?

The one in the back.

GEORGE: That's not for sale.

CUSTOMER: Why not?

Is it the heart of Mother Theresa or something?

GEORGE: It's my mother's heart.

CUSTOMER: Oh.

I'm sorry.

GEORGE: Not your fault.

CUSTOMER: So my choices are between the pediatrician and the public defender?

GEORGE: That's right.

CUSTOMER: I guess I'll take the public defender.

GEORGE: Excellent choice. Have you eaten anything in the past twenty-four hours?

(*She takes out an American Express card.*)

CUSTOMER: No, you're not suppose to eat anything twenty-four hours before major surgery.

GEORGE: That's right.

(*He takes out a hand-held credit card swiper.*)

In case you're worried about appearances, the receipt will simply read 'The Ladder Store'.

(*He swipes her card. Gives it back to her.*)

CUSTOMER: Could I just try the poet's heart? Just to feel what it's like?

GEORGE: I'm afraid that's impossible.

CUSTOMER: Just for a second. I'll pay extra. Please.

(*He takes her card and swipes it again.*)

GEORGE: Fine.

But only for a little while.

4

Under the bridge.
The POET has a sign that reads 'POET WITHOUT HEART, PLEASE HELP'.

POET: Please help me. Please? Spare some change. I can't feel anything. I'm numb. I'm completely numb.

(*The HOOKER walks by.*)

HOOKER: It's you.

POET: It's me. Who are you?

HOOKER: I'm the prostitute whose pimp beat you up.

POET: Hey. How are you?

HOOKER: Can't complain. You?

POET: I still don't feel anything.

HOOKER: What about this?

You worthless two-bit whore!

POET: Nothing, I'm afraid.

HOOKER: That's what T-Bone calls me when I screw
something up.

It usually makes me feel pretty bad.

POET: I'm sorry for you.

HOOKER: Hey.

You felt when T-Bone hit you, right?

POET: I think he cracked a rib.

HOOKER: So you don't have any emotions but you can feel
physical pain.

POET: That's true.

I can feel physical pain.

HOOKER: You want me to hit you?

POET: No thanks.

HOOKER: Come on.

Wouldn't you rather feel pain than nothing?

It's like Faulkner wrote, 'Between grief or nothing, I choose
grief.'

POET: What novel is that from.

HOOKER: 'Wild Palms'. I think it's one of his best.

POET: Personally, I prefer –

(*She hits him in the stomach.*)

HOOKER: Sorry I had to resort to the element of surprise.

POET: It's okay. You've got a good hook.

HOOKER: People say it's my specialty.

(*JEFF walks by eating an ice cream cone.*)

POET: Hey, mister, can you spare some change?

HOOKER: Hey, mister, you looking for a party?

JEFF: Sorry.

I don't have any change and I hate parties.

But you can have the rest of my ice cream cone.

(*JEFF gives the POET the ice cream cone.*)

Chocolate vanilla swirl. It's my favorite.

POET: Thanks.

(*JEFF gives the POET some napkins.*)

JEFF: And some napkins in case it gets too drippy.

Have a great day.

HOOKER: You too, honey.

(*JEFF goes.*)

POET: Do you work on this street?

HOOKER: On Wednesdays. I got some nice regulars over
here.

Nobody tries to beat me up or nothing.

Do you want a blowjob?

POET: I can't afford a blowjob. I live my life in pursuit of truth
and beauty. It doesn't pay very well.

HOOKER: On the house.

It's the least I can do. You look so sad.

POET: Do I?

Sad.

I don't think I'm sad. I'm cold. And wet. Maybe that's
what you see.

HOOKER: Either way you're depressing me. I don't know if I
can work tonight thinking about you like this.

POET: If it would make you feel better, I would accept a
blowjob.

HOOKER: I rent out the back of that Chevy.

POET: Maybe you can make me feel something.

HOOKER: Just relax, honey.

You're in the hands of a seasoned professional.

(*She leads him off toward the Chevy.*)

5

The Ladder Store. There's blood everywhere.
The POET's heart is in.

CUSTOMER: The world is so beautiful. Look at all these
ladders. Before they were just metal and wood and now...
Oh, God. I wish I had the words.

I can feel my past.

I'm six months old. My Mom. She's giving me a bath in
the sink. How beautiful she used to be. Oh no. I've got
soap in my eyes. I'm crying. Mommy! Get the soap out of
my eyes. It stings, Mommy! Why can't she understand me?

GEORGE: Are you okay?

CUSTOMER: I'm twelve. I'm at our summer home in the
hammock. I watch my mother leaving for her walk at
dusk. Fireflies follow her. The moon follows her. I want to
follow her but the hammock is so comfortable. I close my
eyes and dream that Bobby Lafonte and I get married and
have quintuplets with no arms or legs. But I'm not scared. I
wake up and it's cold. Where's my Mom? Mommy?

She doesn't come home from her walk. She died.

I can feel her absence. I can hold it in my hands. It's
tangible.

Can you feel it?

GEORGE: No. I can't.

CUSTOMER: It's right here. It's in this room. Her absence. It's
everywhere.

GEORGE: I think I should take that heart out.

CUSTOMER: Not yet.

Just a little bit longer. Please. I've never felt so much.

6

In the Chevy.
It's post blowjob.

POET: I felt that.

I felt your mouth. And your tongue. And your tongue ring. It was wonderful.

HOOKER: People say it's my specialty.

POET: Let me look at you.

You're so beautiful.

HOOKER: You should have seen me thirty-five years ago.

(*He takes out paper and pen from his pocket.*

He starts to write. He can't.)

POET: Nothing. I can't describe your face. It's like…

Your face is like…

HOOKER: Like a melon. That's what T-Bone says. Like a honeydew melon.

POET: Your face is like –

HOOKER: – a face?

POET: Your face is like a face?

HOOKER: I don't know. You're the poet.

POET: Your legs are like. Your hands are like.

HOOKER: I like it. My ears are like. My hair is like.

POET: I can't describe anything. The world remains. I can't make it new.

Wait!

'When I was a child, the world was younger too.'

HOOKER: That sounds like poetry!

POET: It's doggerel. I'm faking it.

HOOKER: I fake it all the time.

POET: Every syllable has to be felt.

How can I write poetry if I can't feel anything?

HOOKER: If you're good at faking it everybody goes home happy. That's what T-Bone taught me.

POET: What were you thinking about when you gave me that blowjob?

HOOKER: Who I voted for in the last presidential election.

POET: Do you ever have an actual sexual response?

HOOKER: With a John? No.

POET: What about with T-Bone?

HOOKER: Sometimes when T-Bone is real nice to me. He makes me a bubble bath with these special bubbles.

He washes my hair. Dries me off. Paints my toenails.

Sometimes we make love, but sometimes he just holds me.

POET: I want to take a bath in your bathtub.

HOOKER: I don't think T-Bone is gonna wash your hair.

POET: No T-Bone. You.

Bubbles. Warm water. Your hands in my hair.

Please. Let me feel those things.

HOOKER: Let me turn a few tricks and then we'll continue with the pro bono work, okay?

POET: Okay.

HOOKER: Go wait under the bridge.

POET: Don't be long.

HOOKER: I never am.

(*The POET gets out of the Chevy and walks off.*)

Next!

7

The Ladder Store.
CUSTOMER and GEORGE.

CUSTOMER: Look at you. You're so depressed.

GEORGE: No I'm not.

CUSTOMER: Your mother. You miss your mother.

GEORGE: Of course I miss her. She's dead.

CUSTOMER: I can feel your regret. Your guilt.

GEORGE: I'm taking that heart out.

CUSTOMER: You feel like you failed her.

GEORGE: I didn't fail her.

CUSTOMER: You love your brother but you resent having to take care of him.

GEORGE: I would do anything for Jeff.

CUSTOMER: Of course you would, but you resent it.

GEORGE: He's my problem. Let me worry about it, okay?

CUSTOMER: Whoah.

Don't get angry.

GEORGE: Who's angry?

CUSTOMER: You are.

GEORGE: I'm not angry.

CUSTOMER: I beg to differ.

You wear anger like a coat.

You wear it like a second skin.

It's your protection from the world.

From the fear you hold within.

I rhymed!

GEORGE: Shut up!

CUSTOMER: Don't yell at me!

GEORGE: If you don't like my anger then maybe you should stay out of my fucking business!

(*Maybe the CUSTOMER cries out of fear.*)

CUSTOMER: Please take this heart out.

I can't handle it.

GEORGE: I told you it was a waste of time.

CUSTOMER: You were right.

I'm sorry. I'm so sorry.

(*The CUSTOMER hugs GEORGE, crying.*)

Please say you're not angry with me.

GEORGE: I'm not angry with you.

CUSTOMER: Do you mean it?

GEORGE: Yes, I mean it.

CUSTOMER: Don't lie.

GEORGE: I'm not lying.

CUSTOMER: I know you're not, I'm sorry I accused you of that. I'm so sorry.
(*GEORGE holds her. She sobs.*)

8

On the street.
T-BONE.

T-BONE: What's up New Haven?! (*Or wherever the play is being performed.*) Goddamn cold out tonight, huh? My name's T-Bone. I'm a pimp. And let me tell you it was not my first choice of jobs. No sir. I was gonna be a pilot. First time I saw a plane I was seven years old. My Grandma took me to the airport. We ate bologna sandwiches in the parking lot and watched the planes taking off, talking about where they was going. This one's going to Tahiti. That one's going to New Orleans. This one's going to Bermuda.
We talked about all the people on them planes. How happy they was to be going somewhere else.
Ever since then I wanted to be a pilot. Instead I became a pimp. I think about all the places I woulda seen if I had been a pilot. All the clouds. All the oceans. When my Grandma died I spread her ashes at the airport, hoping maybe they would get somewhere good on one of them planes. Tahiti. New Orleans. Bermuda.
I never been on a plane but I'm saving up. Pretty soon I'm gonna get on a plane and never come back. Not ever. Even in my dreams I won't come back.

9

The Ladder Store.
The CUSTOMER has a large bandage over her chest.

CUSTOMER: You were right. This is a much better fit.

I feel so much. I feel my suffering and yours.

But it's not overwhelming. I can control it.

GEORGE: I'm glad you're satisfied.

CUSTOMER: You should talk to Jeff about your mother.

GEORGE: I want to. I've been waiting for the right time.

CUSTOMER: There is no time but *now.*

(*JEFF enters.*)

JEFF: I'm back!

(*GEORGE gives the CUSTOMER a ladder.*)

GEORGE: Well, I'm glad we could find the ladder that fit all of your ladder needs.

CUSTOMER: Me too. Thank you so much. Now I can climb as high as I want.

GEORGE: Goodbye.

(*She hugs GEORGE long and hard.*)

CUSTOMER: Goodbye.

(*She hugs JEFF long and hard and gives him a kiss on the cheek.*)

Take care of each other.

Love each other.

(*She goes.*)

JEFF: Geez, what a weird lady.

GEORGE: How was your lunch?

JEFF: It was great. I had a steak sandwich. Another steak sandwich. And some ice cream.

GEORGE: You've got it all over your face.

JEFF: I do?

GEORGE: Come here.

(*GEORGE dabs a napkin with his spit and cleans JEFF's face.*)

JEFF: That weird, huggy lady forgot her purse.

GEORGE: Shit. I'll be right back.

(*GEORGE runs out with the purse.*)

JEFF: Don't worry about it.

I'll just dust the ladders.

(*JEFF dusts the ladders.*

A MILLIONAIRE like from a silent movie enters. He wears a handsome suit. A top hat. Spats.)

Good afternoon, sir. Welcome to The Ladder Store.

MILLIONAIRE: Good afternoon.

JEFF: Is there any ladder in particular I can help you with? Or are you just browsing?

MILLIONAIRE: Just browsing, thank you.

JEFF: I'll be right here if you need anything. My name is Jeff.

MILLIONAIRE: Thank you, Jeff.

You sure do have a lot of ladders.

JEFF: Yes, sir. Every ladder of today and some from yesterday.

That's our motto. My motto, actually. What do you think?

MILLIONAIRE: About what?

JEFF: The motto.

MILLIONAIRE: I don't like it.

JEFF: What about this one:

'However high you want to go we'll take you there.'

MILLIONAIRE: I don't like that one either.

JEFF: 'For every rung in life we'll hold you up.'

MILLIONAIRE: They aren't very good mottoes, Jeff. I'm sorry.

JEFF: Let me ask you. Do you think they could make a ladder that goes to the moon?

MILLIONAIRE: No.

But you're the ladder expert, Jeff.

JEFF: That's right, I am. And I say yes.

MILLIONAIRE: Then it's settled.

Let me tell you, Jeff, I was sent here looking for a very special ladder.

JEFF: We don't have any ladders to heaven, sir, if that's what
 you mean.

MILLIONAIRE: I'm not looking to go to heaven. I'm looking
 for a very special ladder.

JEFF: I think I know what you're talking about.

MILLIONAIRE: Excellent.

JEFF: You're talking about the GetMeHigher6000. It's very
 special, sir.

 (*GEORGE enters.*)

GEORGE: Is there anything I can help you with, sir?

JEFF: I got this one, Bro.

 He wants the GetMeHigher6000.

 I was just about to tell him all the special features.

MILLIONAIRE: Maybe you can help me. I was sent here
 looking for a very special ladder.

 I hate being on the ground.

GEORGE: I think I can help.

JEFF: I got this one, Bro!

GEORGE: Take lunch, Jeff.

JEFF: I already ate lunch.

GEORGE: Then take a walk.

JEFF: My feet hurt.

 And it's cold outside.

MILLIONAIRE: I can come back if this is an inopportune time.

GEORGE: It's a perfect time, sir.

 Jeff, I need you to leave so I can have a little private time,
 okay?

JEFF: Fine.

 Everybody needs private time. Sometimes I need private
 time, too. I don't even tell you about it. That's how private
 it is.

GEORGE: Here.

 Take some quarters. Go play pinball.

JEFF: The machine's broken.

GEORGE: What about Ms Pac Man?

JEFF: No, that's working.

GEORGE: You love Ms Pac Man.

JEFF: That's true, I do.

> (*JEFF takes the quarters.*)
>
> I'll see you later. Nice to meet you, sir.
>
> I hope my brother can help you find the ladder that will meet all of your particular ladder needs.

MILLIONAIRE: Thank you, Jeff.

> (*JEFF goes.*)

GEORGE: My apologies, sir.

MILLIONAIRE: Am I in the right place for a very special ladder?

GEORGE: Yes, sir. This is the place.

MILLIONAIRE: Excellent.

> (*GEORGE takes out a stethoscope and listens to the MILLIONAIRE's heart.*)

GEORGE: What seems to be the problem?

MILLIONAIRE: When I hold my children, I wish my wife would take them.

> When I make love to my wife I wish I was alone.
>
> When I'm alone I wish I was with my mistress.
>
> When I'm with my mistress I wish I was with my wife.
>
> I own an island. A private plane.
>
> I can buy anything in the world but I can't feel anything.
>
> I want to feel the world, not just own it.

GEORGE: And money is no object?

MILLIONAIRE: No object!

GEORGE: Will you please wait here while I check my inventory.

10

In the bath.
The POET soaks. The HOOKER sits near.

POET: Will you wash my hair again?

HOOKER: You're gonna get a rash if I wash it again.

POET: Please. Just one more time. Pretty please.

HOOKER: Fine.

Just one more time.

(*She washes his hair.*)

POET: Your fingers are so amazing.

HOOKER: People say they're my specialty.

POET: Do you know any lullabies?

My mother used to sing me lullabies in the bath.

HOOKER: My Mom did too.

Until she died.

POET: Your Mom died when you were a child?

HOOKER: When I was four.

POET: That should make me cry.

I'm so sorry I can't cry.

HOOKER: Don't worry about it.

I can't cry either.

POET: That's terrible.

HOOKER: I used to cry when I was working but it would freak
out the customers.

And then I used to cry in my pillow but T-Bone couldn't
sleep and he hit me so I stopped crying altogether.

You still want me to sing?

POET: Only if you want to.

HOOKER: This is from 'Dumbo', the movie.

(*She sings 'Baby Mine' by Ned Washington and Frank Churchill
and washes his hair.*

T-BONE enters and hears her sing the final verse.)

T-BONE: What's going on here?

HOOKER: This is a client. I'm getting paid.

POET: You said this was pro bono.

T-BONE: Pro what?

HOOKER: Shhhh.

T-BONE: You're washing his hair. You're singing our song.

HOOKER: That's what he wanted, T-Bone.

You told me do whatever they want.

T-BONE: This is our bathtub.

This is our special place, baby.

HOOKER: I know, baby. Don't get angry.

POET: T-bone. Perhaps I could explain.

T-BONE: Shut up!

(*T-BONE hits the POET in the head.*)

POET: I can feel that.

Hit me again!

(*T-BONE hits him again.*)

Now that's what the doctor ordered.

HOOKER: Don't hit him.

T-BONE: Don't tell me what to do, baby!

(*T-BONE hits her in the stomach.*)

You brought a John to our special place. You washed his hair. Why?

Can you tell me that?

HOOKER: I told him how you wash my hair and he wanted to feel like me.

T-BONE: You told him!

HOOKER: Baby, I'm sorry.

T-BONE: That's private, baby. That's our private time.

(*T-BONE hits her in the stomach.*)

You know I hate to hurt you.

HOOKER: I know you do.

T-BONE: It eats me up inside. Like a virus. Like a plague.

HOOKER: I shouldn't have brought him here.

T-BONE: You're goddamn right.

You shouldn't have brought this little bitch to our tub.

Go outside, baby.

HOOKER: Do I have to?

T-BONE: You know you do.

HOOKER: Bye. I'm sorry.

POET: That's okay.

I felt so much.

(*She goes.*)

T-BONE: What were you thinking coming here getting into my tub? That is just about the stupidest motherfucking thing I ever heard.

POET: T-Bone. I'm sorry.

T-BONE: Don't call me 'T-Bone', bitch.

Call me 'sir'.

POET: I'm sorry, sir.

I wanted to come here and feel the warm water. Her hands in my hair.

This might sound strange but I don't have a heart.

T-BONE: You think I have a heart, motherfucker?

Nobody can have a heart in this world and survive.

POET: Can I tell you a story?

T-BONE: Is it a scary story? 'Cause I hate scary stories.

POET: It's not a scary story.

T-BONE: It better not be.

POET: It's about my heart.

One day I was walking by the river, and a man jumped me and took my heart…

11

The Ladder Store.
GEORGE has the cooler.

GEORGE: This is the heart of a pediatrician.

This heart would let you feel an enormous sense of compassion. And deserved righteousness.

MILLIONAIRE: What about that one?

GEORGE: I see you have a very good eye.

(*GEORGE takes the POET's heart out of the cooler.*)

MILLIONAIRE: Is it a special heart?

GEORGE: This is the heart of a poet.

MILLIONAIRE: I hate poetry. All those rhymes.

I don't need thirteen ways of looking at a blackbird.
I need one.

(*The HOOKER holds up a large picture of a blackbird.*)

There it is, a fucking blackbird.

GEORGE: This heart would let you see the world with a profound clarity. You'd see people as they truly are. And it would give you a sense of empathy that borders on the clairvoyant.

MILLIONAIRE: I'm a businessman.

Don't give me that emotional flim-flam sales pitch.

GEORGE: Do you know about cars?

MILLIONAIRE: I own fifty-two of them.

GEORGE: This is the Rolls Royce of hearts.

MILLIONAIRE: You got yourself a deal.

(*They shake hands.*)

GEORGE: Excellent.

When would you like to begin?

MILLIONAIRE: As soon as possible.

GEORGE: I could perform the transplant this afternoon.

MILLIONAIRE: Just a second.

(*He dials a cell-phone.*)

Hey, it's me.

Cancel everything.

Did I stutter? Everything!

(*He hangs up the phone.*)

Sorry, about that. I'm ready.

GEORGE: Have you eaten anything in the past twenty-four hours?

MILLIONAIRE: I had a hot dog.

GEORGE: You're not supposed to eat anything before major surgery.

MILLIONAIRE: It was a tiny hot dog. More like a cocktail wiener than a hot dog.

GEORGE: Anything else?

MILLIONAIRE: And a knish. Some salami. A gyro. Curly fries. A waffle. Two waffles.

GEORGE: We'll perform the transplant tomorrow.

MILLIONAIRE: Please. Please do it today.

I might change my mind tomorrow. Please. I can't live like this anymore.

GEORGE: It's not safe.

MILLIONAIRE: Please. I'm on my fucking knees here. What do you want? Stock options?

Women? I know these Philippine Siamese twins –

GEORGE: That won't be necessary, sir.

MILLIONAIRE: Are you sure? You could do one and I could do the other and it'd be like a double-decker corned beef sandwich.

Did I mention I also ate a corned beef sandwich?

GEORGE: No.

MILLIONAIRE: Well, I did.

GEORGE: Look I think –

MILLIONAIRE: I'll pay. I'll pay whatever you want. You can take care of yourself and your idiot brother for the rest of your life. What do you say?

GEORGE: May I take your top hat, please? I'm going to put this mask over your nose and mouth. Just breathe normally.

(*MILLIONAIRE inhales very, very hard.*)

I said normally!

MILLIONAIRE: Sorry, I was trying to get a buzz

GEORGE: Just count backwards from ten.

MILLIONAIRE: 10, 9, 8,

7.

7.

7.

(*He passes out. GEORGE takes out the POET's heart.*)

12

On the street.
The HOOKER is working.
JEFF walks by.

JEFF: Hello.

HOOKER: You're the guy who hates parties and loves ice cream, right?

JEFF: You remember me!

HOOKER: I remember you.

JEFF: I was watching how you stand out here and people come up and talk to you so I stood on a corner for an hour and a half but nobody came up to talk to me.

HOOKER: I'm sorry.

JEFF: You must be an excellent conversationalist.

HOOKER: People say it's my specialty.

JEFF: Will you have a conversation with me?

HOOKER: Of course.

What do you want to talk about?

JEFF: I don't know.

You're the professional.

You should probably pick the topic.

HOOKER: It sure is cold out, huh?

JEFF: It sure is.

When I was standing on the corner waiting for somebody to talk to I lost all the feeling in my toes and had to soak them in hot water for fifteen minutes before the feeling came back.

Do your toes ever lose their feeling?

HOOKER: Sometimes.

JEFF: I guess it's a professional hazard.

HOOKER: You get used to it.

(*Silence.*)

JEFF: That wasn't a very good conversation.

HOOKER: I'm sorry.

JEFF: It's not your fault.

You're probably just tired.

HOOKER: I've been talking a lot today.

JEFF: Can we try again?

HOOKER: Sure.

What kind of work do you do?

JEFF: I'm Manager at The Ladder Store.

HOOKER: Is that interesting?

JEFF: Oh yeah.

I sell ladders and my brother sells widgets shaped like human hearts.

He brought in this special widget from a poet and once he unloads it he wants to sell The Ladder Store but I'm like, 'Without us how are people going to get cats out of trees?'

HOOKER: Or get footballs off garages.

JEFF: Exactly.

You should drop by the store sometime. I'll show you all the latest ladder models.

It's incredible where the industry is going.

HOOKER: Listen –

JEFF: – I am sooo good at listening. That and leadership which is surprising because I don't think of myself as a natural born leader.

HOOKER: I have to go inside now.

JEFF: Are your toes getting cold?

HOOKER: I can barely feel them.

JEFF: Thanks for the conversation.

HOOKER: I'm sorry it was so short.

JEFF: It's not the length that matters, right?

HOOKER: That's right.

(She kisses him on the cheek and goes inside.
JEFF giggles to himself and walks away.)

13

In the bathtub.

POET: ...and then I wandered the streets cold and hungry and numb.

T-BONE: That's a fucking sad story.

POET: I know.

T-BONE: You didn't warn me it was gonna be so fucking sad.

POET: I'm sorry.

T-BONE: A heads-up woulda been appreciated.

(The HOOKER enters.)

Come here, baby.

(T-BONE holds the HOOKER and cries into her shoulder.)

I'm sorry.

HOOKER: I know you are.

T-BONE: I'm so sorry!

(He sobs.)

HOOKER: Baby. I know where this poet's heart is.

T-BONE / POET: Where?

HOOKER: Over at The Ladder Store.

The ladders are just a front.

It's actually a black market heart operation.

T-BONE: I knew that.

I was thinking about trading up. This heart I got feels too damn much.

I can barely run my business.

HOOKER: So?

T-BONE: So? I'm thinking it over.

HOOKER: No.

Let's go steal the poet's heart.

T-BONE: That sounds dangerous, baby. You know I don't like
danger!

HOOKER: We can do something good for somebody else.

POET: It would mean a lot to me, T-Bone.

T-BONE: Fuck it.

Get my gun, baby.

Let's go get that heart back!

(*The HOOKER kisses T-BONE and runs out.*)

POET: Thank you, T-Bone.

T-BONE: Don't tell nobody about this.

POET: I won't.

T-BONE: I got a reputation to uphold.

POET: I won't say a word.

T-BONE: Hey, even though that was a fucking sad story it was
still pretty good.

POET: Thank you, T-Bone.

T-BONE: Hang tight.

We'll be back with your heart ASAP.

You got enough hot water?

You don't want any more bubbles or nothing?

POET: Some more bubbles would be great.

T-BONE: Here you go.

(*T-BONE puts more bubbles in.*)

POET: Thank you, T-Bone.

T-BONE: Don't mention it.

Back in a jiff.

(*T-BONE goes.*)

POET: Bye.

(*He blows on the bubbles. Sings or plays 'Baby Mine'.
Finds a rubber ducky and plays with it.*)

14

The Ladder Store.

After the surgery. There's blood everywhere. The MILLIONAIRE has a large bandage over his chest. He is still lying down unconscious. GEORGE is throwing the old heart away.

T-BONE and the HOOKER enter with pantyhose over their faces. T-BONE has a gun.

T-BONE: This is a stick-up.

HOOKER: Everybody put your motherfucking hands in the air or I swear to Christ I will pop asses in everybody's cap.

T-BONE: Easy, baby.

It's just the one guy.

(*GEORGE puts his hands up.*)

HOOKER: Tell him to put his motherfucking hands up.

GEORGE: I can hear you.

My hands are already up.

HOOKER: Tell him to put on the motherfucking handcuffs!

T-BONE: Put these on.

(*T-BONE gives GEORGE handcuffs. GEORGE puts them on.*)

GEORGE: I recognize you. I was going to give you a deal on that dentist's heart.

T-BONE: You don't know me.

HOOKER: You don't know him.

(*T-BONE hits him.*)

GEORGE: You're right. I don't know you.

(*JEFF enters.*)

JEFF: George!

I got a new high score on Ms Pac Man and had the most amazing conversation.

GEORGE: That's great, Jeff.

JEFF: Hello, are you two here for a ladder?

T-BONE: We're here for the poet's heart.

JEFF: There are no hearts here, sir, only ladders and widgets.

HOOKER: Tell him to shut the fuck up and put on the
  motherfucking handcuffs.

T-BONE: Put these on.

  (*T-BONE throws him handcuffs.*)

JEFF: No thank you. I don't like playing games with handcuffs.

T-BONE: This ain't no game.

HOOKER: Tell him I will put a bullet through his
  motherfucking eye.

GEORGE: Put on the handcuffs, Jeff.

  (*JEFF puts on the handcuffs.*)

JEFF: Should I close my eyes?

GEORGE: Yes, Jeff. Close your eyes.

  (*JEFF closes his eyes hard.*)

T-BONE: Where's the heart, bitch?

HOOKER: Where is the motherfucking heart?

JEFF: Hey. I recognize you. You're the great conversationalist.

T-BONE: Stay back!

HOOKER: You must be confusing me with somebody else.

JEFF: We had a conversation about how cold it was and The
  Ladder Store.

  Don't you remember?

T-BONE: Do you know this guy?

HOOKER: Of course not.

  You must be making a mistake, motherfucker.

JEFF: I don't make mistakes.

HOOKER: Listen.

  I have a cousin who's a great conversationalist and we
  have the exact same voice.

  Maybe you're thinking of her.

JEFF: Maybe.

  But I doubt it.

T-BONE: Enough chit-chat.

  Where's the heart?

JEFF: How should I know? My eyes are closed.

GEORGE: It's in the fat man's chest.

T-BONE: Then the fat man's coming with us.

(T-BONE picks up the MILLIONAIRE.)

Damn!

What this motherfucker eat?

GEORGE: He had a cocktail wiener, some salami, a gyro, curly fries, two waffles and a double-decker corned beef sandwich.

HOOKER: Count backwards from a million, motherfuckers!

JEFF: I would love to, but I don't know any numbers higher than fifty.

HOOKER: Fine. Then count backwards from fifty very motherfucking slowly.

(T-BONE and the HOOKER exit, T-BONE huffing and puffing carrying the MILLIONAIRE.)

JEFF: Gotcha.

Fifty, forty-nine, forty-eight, forty-seven.

George, what comes after forty-seven?

GEORGE: Forty-six.

JEFF: Of course, forty-six!

GEORGE: You can open your eyes now, Jeff.

JEFF: This game is fun.

GEORGE: Jeff, I lied to you.

JEFF: Should I keep counting? Forty-five, forty-four…

GEORGE: No. I don't sell widgets, Jeff.

I sell hearts.

JEFF: Human hearts?

GEORGE: Yes, human hearts.

JEFF: You're not supposed to lie.

That's against the rules.

GEORGE: I know, Jeff. I'm sorry.

JEFF: I don't like this game anymore.

(JEFF picks his handcuffs. He's free.)

GEORGE: How did you do that?

JEFF: You've got your secrets. I've got mine.

15

The bathtub.

T-BONE pours water on the MILLIONAIRE, who is handcuffed in the bathtub.

The HOOKER, T-BONE and the POET all wear pantyhose over their faces. Maybe the HOOKER wears fishnet stockings.

T-BONE: Rise and shine, buttercup.

MILLIONAIRE: Do I have a new heart? Did it work?

POET: How do you feel?

MILLIONAIRE: I feel sore.

POET: Sore. What else?

MILLIONAIRE: Uncomfortable. I'm handcuffed in a bathtub.

HOOKER: Is that your heart?

POET: I'm not sure.

MILLIONAIRE: It reminds me of when I was a little boy. And how the world seemed so huge. I remember when my feet wouldn't touch the ground from chairs, and how I could hide underneath tables. There was so much mystery. The world was so scary. But now the world seems so small. I can't hide anywhere.

POET: That's my heart.

T-BONE: You sure?

(*The MILLIONAIRE is crying.*)

POET: I'm sure.

T-BONE: Shut him up.

MILLIONAIRE: Your eyes.

My God. I see my mother in them. Her eyes smiled. They were like strawberries! Mother!

(*The HOOKER puts a sock in his mouth. He cries. And laughs. Because of all the joy in the world but because that joy makes you so sad sometimes.*)

T-BONE: You sure you want that back?

POET: Some people can handle it better than others.

(*The MILLIONAIRE spits out the sock.*)

MILLIONAIRE: The sun is an orb that lights my way

The moon is a rock at which I bay.

(*He bays, like a wolf.*)

POET: I used to bay.

T-BONE: Shut him up.

(*The HOOKER puts the sock back in.*)

There's nothing in the world that should make a man bay like that.

POET: Of course there is. The world is filled with so many miracles.

HOOKER: I had a customer who made me bay.

I didn't like it.

MILLIONAIRE: Mmmmmmhhmmm.

HOOKER: He wants to say something.

T-BONE: What?

(*HOOKER takes out the sock.*)

MILLIONAIRE: My father. He didn't love me. I don't think he could love anything in the entire world.

T-BONE: So what? I never even had a father.

MILLIONAIRE: You didn't, did you?

T-BONE: Never even met the sonofabitch.

MILLIONAIRE: I'm so sorry.

T-BONE: Left my Momma in an alley where she died giving birth to me. My Grandma told me he used to dress up like Santa Claus for the Salvation Army so at Christmas I asked every motherfucker clanging a bell if they was my Daddy.

MILLIONAIRE: That's the saddest thing I have ever heard.

(*He cries.*)

T-BONE: Are you crying for me?

MILLIONAIRE: Do you mind?

T-BONE: Nah. I guess not.

MILLIONAIRE: Why don't you cry with me?

HOOKER: You can cry, T-Bone. Don't be shy.

T-BONE: You won't tell nobody?

POET: Of course not.

HOOKER: Cross my heart and hope to die.

> (*T-BONE sobs hysterically, for all of the people he's lost, and for all of the people he will never know but seem lost to him anyway. He finishes.*)

T-BONE: That felt pretty good.

> Now let's get that heart out.
>
> (*HOOKER puts sock in.*)
>
> Get my scalpel, baby.
>
> (*The HOOKER gives him a scalpel.*)

POET: I can't watch.

> I'm gonna get some air.
>
> (*The POET goes outside.*)

HOOKER: I love the way blood looks.

T-BONE: This might sting a little bit.

> (*The MILLIONAIRE is yelling into his sock.*)

HOOKER: He wants to say something, T-Bone.

T-BONE: I'm gonna guess he doesn't want me to cut into his chest with an old rusty scalpel.

> Am I close?

HOOKER: Let him talk, T-Bone.

> Everybody deserves some last words.

T-BONE: Fine.

> You got any last words?
>
> (*HOOKER takes the sock out.*)

MILLIONAIRE: Before I got this heart, I was a very wealthy businessman.

HOOKER: Weird last words.

MILLIONAIRE: I can pay you. I'll pay you not to take this heart out.

T-BONE: How much are we talking?

> Because it's not like I'm in the poorhouse, here.
>
> I'm also a businessman.

HOOKER: That's right, baby.

> (*They kiss.*)

MILLIONAIRE: How about ten million dollars?

T-BONE: You serious?

MILLIONAIRE: You can call the bank right now.

    We'll get a wire transfer into your account.

T-BONE: I don't exactly have a bank account.

HOOKER: He doesn't believe in banks.

T-BONE: I don't believe in banks.

MILLIONAIRE: Then how about cash?

T-BONE: Ten million in cash?

MILLIONAIRE: It'll take one phone call.

T-BONE: Is it long distance?

MILLIONAIRE: I'll pay for the call.

T-BONE: You got yourself a deal.

    (*T-BONE shakes the MILLIONAIRE's hand, even though the MILLIONAIRE's hand is in handcuffs.*)

16

The Ladder Store.
Nobody's in handcuffs. GEORGE shows JEFF different hearts.

GEORGE: This is the heart of a pediatrician.

    This is the heart of a kindergarten teacher.

    (*JEFF raises his hand, like in school.*)

    Jeff?

JEFF: What's that one?

GEORGE: You have a good eye.

    This is a very special heart, Jeff.

    This is Mom's heart.

JEFF: Mom's heart?

GEORGE: I kept it after she died.

JEFF: Were you going to sell it?

GEORGE: Of course not.

JEFF: Good. Because this is a private, family heirloom.

GEORGE: I want you to do something for me, Jeff.

JEFF: Should I close my eyes and count backwards from fifty?

GEORGE: I want you to put Mom's heart in my chest.

Because I can't remember her anymore.

I see pictures and remember the pictures. I don't remember her.

JEFF: I don't remember her, either.

GEORGE: So let's do this.

For both of us.

We can remember.

Please.

JEFF: Okay, George. I'll help you put Mom's heart in your chest so we can remember.

(*GEORGE hugs JEFF.*)

GEORGE: Thank you, Jeff.

JEFF: The only problem is I don't know how to perform heart surgery.

GEORGE: I'll talk you through it.

It's a piece of cake.

JEFF: What kind of cake?

GEORGE: Angel food cake.

JEFF: Mmmm.

I love angel food cake.

GEORGE: I know you do, Jeff.

I know you do.

17

The bathtub.
The MILLIONAIRE is in the bathtub. The POET sits nearby.

POET: Tell me what you feel.

MILLIONAIRE: Do you want me to?

POET: Yes. I want to remember.

MILLIONAIRE: I feel my wrists. They hurt. And I think about everyone who's been in chains before. However justly or unjustly, the pain is always the same. And I feel your numbness.

And I feel T-Bone's gratitude. And I feel sorry for myself. Because I betrayed you. I paid them to let me keep your heart.

POET: I don't blame you.

MILLIONAIRE: You should.

POET: If I could feel anything maybe I would but I don't so don't worry about it.

MILLIONAIRE: This heart has a memory. You led a life of extraordinary beauty. Not concerned with the cares of the world, but with the truth of it. The nature of your soul. The quest for beauty.

POET: I tried to.

MILLIONAIRE: You did. You really did. It's beautiful.

(*T-BONE and HOOKER come in with a suitcase full of money.*)

T-BONE: My Grandma told me never to trust a man in handcuffs. But you were right. You were right as rain.

MILLIONAIRE: You got all ten million?

T-BONE: To the penny!

(*He dumps it on the floor.*)

MILLIONAIRE: That money never gave me anything but grief.

I'm glad it makes you happy.

T-BONE: We're getting on an airplane and flying to Bermuda, baby.

Shit. We're gonna buy Bermuda!

(*They air kiss.*)

MILLIONAIRE: Will you let me go now, please?

POET: His wrists hurt.

He feels the pain of everyone who's been in chains before.

However justly or unjustly, the pain is always the same.

T-BONE: I'm afraid I can't let you go.

MILLIONAIRE: Why not?

T-BONE: You just gave me ten million dollars. Mr Johnny Law might see your largesse as extortion.

HOOKER: Let him go, T-Bone.

T-BONE: Shut up, baby.

(*T-BONE hits her toe.*)

MILLIONAIRE: The money means nothing to me, T-Bone. I don't care about it.

T-BONE: I'm sorry.

(*He takes out a gun and points it to the MILLIONAIRE's head.*)

POET: Please. That's my heart.

HOOKER: Please, baby.

MILLIONAIRE: I give you my word, T-Bone. Please. Let me live.

T-BONE: You promise on the soul of my dead Momma you won't try to get this money back?

MILLIONAIRE: I promise on the soul of your dead Momma.

(*Puts the gun away.*)

T-BONE: Fuck it. Today, everybody hit their number.

Baby, undo the handcuffs.

MILLIONAIRE: Thank you, T-Bone.

POET: Thank you.

T-BONE: Get the fuck out of here. Both of ya.

(*As the MILLIONAIRE's getting out of the bathtub.*)

T-BONE: Can you hurry up, please.

I would appreciate some private time with my money and my baby.

MILLIONAIRE: I'm going as fast as I can.

POET: It's very slippery.

(*MILLIONAIRE is out of tub.*)

T-BONE: You want a towel?

MILLIONAIRE: No, I'll drip dry but thank you.

HOOKER: Goodbye.

POET: Goodbye.

MILLIONAIRE: Goodbye.

T-BONE: Goodbye.

HOOKER: That was real nice of you, baby.

(*T-BONE kisses her. A big wet and sloppy R-rated kiss.*)

T-BONE: Let me give you a bath, baby.

HOOKER: But I'm not dirty.

T-BONE: Come on, baby, let me wash your hair.

HOOKER: Only if you sing.

T-BONE: Fine. I'll sing.

HOOKER: You got yourself a deal.

(*She gets in the bath.*
And then somewhere else onstage we see the POET and the
MILLIONAIRE.
They're not near the bathtub, they're under the bridge, near the
river, or walking towards one or both.)

POET: Will you do me a favor?

MILLIONAIRE: I will try my very best.

POET: Will you hit me?

I can't feel anything except physical pleasure or pain.

So it's either you hit me or give me a blowjob.

MILLIONAIRE: Those are my only two choices?

POET: I guess a handjob would be okay but there's so much
chafing.

MILLIONAIRE: Let me think about it.

POET: Take your time.

(*Meanwhile, the HOOKER has gotten into the tub.*)

T-BONE: You ain't ever gonna have to ho again, baby.

We're going to Bermuda and everything's gonna be
different.

HOOKER: Sing our song, baby.

(*T-BONE sings 'Baby Mine' and washes her hair. This continues*
under the rest of the Act.)

MILLIONAIRE: I decided to hit you. Are you ready?

POET: As ready as I'll ever be.

MILLIONAIRE: Here goes.

(*The MILLIONAIRE hits the POET.*
The POET coughs.)

POET: Thank you. You got a pretty good jab.

MILLIONAIRE: Do you really think so?

POET: You're not exactly Sonny Listen, but together we'll
   work on it.

MILLIONAIRE: Together?

POET: Together.

   (*And now we're at The Ladder Store, without having lost either
   of the other two threads.*

   After the surgery.

   JEFF is in a doctor outfit covered in blood.

   GEORGE has a huge bandage over his chest.)

JEFF: Wake up.

   Wake up.

   (*GEORGE wakes up.*

   Looks around.)

GEORGE: (*As Mom, but not necessarily in the voice.*) George?

JEFF: No.

   It's me, Jeff.

GEORGE: Jeff. My baby.

JEFF: Your baby.

GEORGE: Give your Momma a hug.

   (*They hug.*)

   END OF ACT ONE

Act Two

18

The beach. Bermuda.
We hear the sound of the surf.
T-BONE and HOOKER in beach clothes. Zinc on their noses.
The HOOKER wears an absurd amount of gaudy jewelry.
A cooler of beer and the suitcase of money are close by.

T-BONE: Bermuda!

Pink sand. Blue water. Bluest thing I ever seen.

My Momma's eyes was blue. I never seen 'em except in pictures. She always looked away from the camera. Hated having her picture taken. She was so shy.

Waiter!

(*A WAITER enters.*)

WAITER: Yes, sir?

T-BONE: Take our picture.

WAITER: Very good, sir.

T-BONE: And get the water in the background.

Get the blue.

(*The WAITER lines up a shot.*)

WAITER: Say cheese.

T-BONE: Fuck that. We're rich. We say formagge.

WAITER: Say formagge.

T-BONE / HOOKER: Formagge!

(*The WAITER snaps a picture.*)

19

Under the bridge.
The MILLIONAIRE is warming himself by a fire in a trash can. It's
early morning.

MILLIONAIRE: Did you sleep?

POET: I don't know. Maybe a little. You?

MILLIONAIRE: All through the night.

POET: Go figure.

MILLIONAIRE: I had the most amazing dreams.

Do you want to hear about them?

POET: Not really.

MILLIONAIRE: There was one when I was in a hot-air balloon
in outer space. I don't know how I could breathe but that's
the wonderful thing about dreams. There doesn't have to
be a reason for things.

I was looking down at the earth. I could see the Great Wall
of China. I tried to see you but everything was so far away.
It made me feel very small, and insignificant. And alone.
Like the stars.

The stars look so close but they're actually billions of miles
apart. Isn't that sad?

POET: Shut up, will you?

MILLIONAIRE: Somebody needs a tickle.

(*He tickles the POET.*)

POET: Cut it out, asshole.

MILLIONAIRE: You are so cranky in the mornings. Anybody
ever tell you that?

POET: Nope. That's a new one.

MILLIONAIRE: It's the morning. The world begins again.

The laws of nature are still the laws we knew yesterday.
Gravity. Entropy. Photosynthesis.

And even though we might feel alone like the stars we get
to be near each other.

(*The POET breaks bottle and cuts himself.*)

MILLIONAIRE: I hate it when you have to do that. But the red is so beautiful.

It's not enough anymore.

POET: This isn't enough anymore.

MILLIONAIRE: What more could you do besides cut off a limb.

POET: That's an idea.

MILLIONAIRE: I was joking.

POET: Seriously. Cut off my thumbs.

MILLIONAIRE: I will not.

POET: Or better yet. Cut out my eyes. It'll be really Greek.

MILLIONAIRE: I'm ready to give you that blowjob. I've been practicing on a carrot. You won't even feel my teeth.

POET: I don't want it anymore.

MILLIONAIRE: Then let me give you back your heart.

I can't handle feeling this much.

POET: I don't want it anymore.

You sound like a retard: 'I dreamt I was in a hot-air balloon floating above the earth.'

MILLIONAIRE: Don't mock me.

POET: 'Aren't stars sad? Aren't plants beautiful? Gravity. Entropy. Blah blah blah.

(The POET begins packing his things in a hobo knapsack.)

MILLIONAIRE: What are you doing?

POET: I'm sick of your shit.

I'll find somebody who will help me out.

(As the POET is getting ready to leave, the MILLIONAIRE hits him over the head with a brick or rock or something heavy.)

Now we're talking.

Give me some more of that sugar.

MILLIONAIRE: This isn't for your pleasure.

(The MILLIONAIRE hits him again.

The POET gets pleasure from it.)

I'm trying to knock you out.

(The MILLIONAIRE hits him again.

More pleasure.)

It's much more difficult to do than it looks in movies.

(*The MILLIONAIRE hits the POET again. A little pleasure, but then he's knocked out.*)

You'll thank me later.

I promise.

(*The MILLIONAIRE drags the body off.*)

20

The Ladder Store.

JEFF and GEORGE. Maybe GEORGE wears a dress and some pearls.

JEFF: Tell me about my childhood. What was I like as a baby?

GEORGE: (*As Mom.*) You didn't make a peep.

Your brother George. He made all sorts of racket, and had diarrhea up the wazoo.

Your father and I almost didn't have another baby.

JEFF: So why did you have me?

GEORGE: Because I don't think anybody should be an only child.

I didn't want him to be alone. So I gave you to him.

And then you turned out to be such a sweet baby, Jeff.

You didn't make a peep and never had diarrhea. Not even once.

JEFF: Who did you love more?

Me or George?

GEORGE: How could I choose?

A mother doesn't have favorites.

JEFF: But you treated us differently.

GEORGE: That's because God made you differently.

JEFF: You gave him all the attention.

GEORGE: Everybody gave George attention.

He had his name in the papers.

He was going somewhere.

JEFF: And I was slow.

GEORGE: And you were slow.

But that doesn't mean I loved you any less, Jeff.

You understand, don't you, baby?

JEFF: I understand.

GEORGE: Will you be a good boy and fix your mother a drink, please?

My throat is parched.

JEFF: No, ma'am.

Drinking's what killed you the first time.

GEORGE: Jeff.

I won't ask you again.

Fix me a drink.

JEFF: Fine.

But just one.

GEORGE: Just one teensy-weensy drink.

My throat is parched.

(*JEFF begins to make a drink.*)

But since I only get one, you better make it a double.

21

Bermuda. The beach.
T-BONE is in the sun.
The HOOKER comes on with the WAITER. He slips her some money.

HOOKER: Thanks, honey. I'll see you later.

WAITER: See you later.

(*He leaves.*)

T-BONE: Did you just turn a trick?

HOOKER: Yeah, here.

(*She gives him most of the money.*)

T-BONE: Baby, this is not a working vacation. You don't have to ho no more. You are my girlfriend. I am your boyfriend.

HOOKER: That means I can keep all the money.

(*She takes all the money back.*)

T-BONE: It also means you don't have to ho anymore. We're
    rich, baby. We're millionaires.

HOOKER: What if I want to?

T-BONE: You wanna ho?

HOOKER: I'm a people person.

T-BONE: This is the good life, baby. We can buy anything.
    What do you want? A Lexus? A diamond tiara?

HOOKER: You already bought me so much. With all this
    jewelry, I'm five pounds heavier.

T-BONE: I don't want all this money if I can't spend it on you,
    baby.

HOOKER: I don't know what to tell you. I ain't no rich lady
    sipping champagne.

    I like working, T-Bone.

T-BONE: You didn't mind being a ho? And me being your pimp?

HOOKER: You treated me better than anybody's ever treated
    me. You made me feel special.

    With all this money, people say, 'Morning, ma'am' and
    hold doors for me.

    Nobody ever held a door open for me. I don't feel like
    myself.

T-BONE: You're not happy?

HOOKER: I'm happy, baby. But I want to work. Will you let
    me work?

T-BONE: If that's what you want.

HOOKER: I'll still give you eighty percent.

T-BONE: Make it thirty.

HOOKER: Thirty? Thanks, baby.

    (*She kisses him.*

    Her beeper goes off.)

    Shit. I got a two-thirty. I'll see you later.

    (*She leaves.*)

T-BONE: See you later.

22

The Ladder Store.
The MILLIONAIRE drags the body of the POET into the store.
GEORGE has a Martini.

JEFF: Good afternoon. Welcome to the Ladder Store.

MILLIONAIRE: Good afternoon.

GEORGE: (*As Mom.*) Can I fix you a cocktail?

MILLIONAIRE: No thank you.

    I need to give this poet his heart back.

JEFF: Is there a problem with the heart?

MILLIONAIRE: No.

    But he needs it more than I do.

JEFF: I understand.

    Have you eaten anything today?

MILLIONAIRE: No.

GEORGE: You must be starving.

    Let me fix you a pot roast.

JEFF: He can't eat anything, Mom.

    He's going into major surgery.

GEORGE: Just a little casserole?

JEFF: No casserole.

GEORGE: A soufflé.

JEFF: Nothing.

GEORGE: Fine!

JEFF: (*To MILLIONAIRE.*) What was the last thing you ate?

MILLIONAIRE: Yesterday I ate half a burrito somebody threw out.

    And some cat food.

JEFF: But nothing today.

MILLIONAIRE: No. I couldn't find any food.

    I checked three different dumpsters.

JEFF: What about him? What did he last eat?

MILLIONAIRE: He doesn't eat. He's too depressed.

GEORGE: He wouldn't be depressed if he could taste my
soufflé.

JEFF: Mom.

I need you to be quiet for a minute, okay?

GEORGE: Excuse me for trying to feed a starving depressed
homeless person!

JEFF: I just need a little private time.

Why don't you go make yourself another drink.

GEORGE: Now that's an idea!

(*GEORGE makes another drink.*)

JEFF: Are you sure you want to give this poet his heart back?

It's a very rare thing.

Like getting an extra life on Ms Pac Man.

MILLIONAIRE: I'm sure.

Just let me say goodbye to this world of mystery.

JEFF: Take your time.

MILLIONAIRE: Goodbye world of mystery,

of sleep and autumn,

of gold and laughter,

of fog and kisses.

Goodbye world without pretense,

without borders,

without beginnings,

without endings,

without death.

Goodbye. Goodbye.

JEFF: That's beautiful.

Now just lie down and count backwards from ten if you
can count that high.

(*The MILLIONAIRE lies down.*

JEFF puts the gas mask over his face.)

MILLIONAIRE: 10, 9, 9, 9.

(*He's out.*

GEORGE comes back in with a fresh cocktail.)

JEFF: Mom, get my scrubs and my scalpel.

We've got a heart transplant to perform.

GEORGE: You sound so grown up when you talk like that, Jeff.

JEFF: I am grown up.

GEORGE: I'll go and get your scalpel and your scrubs, which make your butt look so cute, by the way.

(*GEORGE slaps JEFF on the ass.*)

JEFF: Mom!

GEORGE: What?

Can't your mother have a little fun?

(*GEORGE exits.*

JEFF is confused.)

23

Bermuda.

T-BONE drinks an umbrella drink. HOOKER walks by.

T-BONE: Hey, baby.

HOOKER: You looking for a party?

T-BONE: Baby. It's me.

HOOKER: Sorry, T-Bone. I'm in business mode.

T-BONE: I got an appointment for us to go parasailing.

HOOKER: I got no time, T-Bone. Business is booming.

T-BONE: Do you like your diamond tiara?

HOOKER: I love it. But I gotta give it back.

T-BONE: Why?

HOOKER: It was getting caught in clients' zippers when I was giving blowjobs.

T-BONE: Whatever's best for business.

HOOKER: I knew you would understand.

(*Her beeper goes off.*)

I would love to catch up right now, but I gotta run. Have fun at the beach, T-Bone.

Don't forget to wear your sunscreen!

T-BONE: I won't.

(*She goes.*)

Waiter!

(*The WAITER enters.*)

WAITER: Yes, sir.

T-BONE: Get me a strawberry daiquiri.

WAITER: Right away, Mr Bone.

T-BONE: And a pina colada. Two pina coladas.

WAITER: Right away, sir.

T-BONE: And some macadamia nuts. I love macadamia nuts.

WAITER: Right away.

T-BONE: And take my picture.

WAITER: With just you?

T-BONE: Do you want to be in it?

WAITER: It's resort policy.

We're not supposed to be in pictures with the guests.

T-BONE: Then just me and the ocean.

WAITER: Very good, sir. Say formagge.

T-BONE: Fuck that. I'm not gonna say nothing. I'm not even gonna smile.

(*WAITER takes the picture. T-BONE is not smiling.*)

Here you go.

(*T-BONE hands the WAITER some money.*)

WAITER: This is a thousand dollars, sir.

T-BONE: I know what it is.

Go get yourself a blowjob from my whore!

I get thirty percent. I'm rich.

What's the difference?

WAITER: I'll be right back with the daquiri, the two pina coladas, and the macadamia nuts.

T-BONE: Maybe when you come back, we can have a conversation.

WAITER: What would we talk about?

T-BONE: Whatever you want. You could pick the topic.

WAITER: It's resort policy. We're not supposed to have conversations with the guests.

T-BONE: Fine. Then just the drinks and the nuts.

WAITER: Very good, sir.

(*WAITER bows and goes.*)

T-BONE: My Momma never saw the ocean. She lived five miles from the ocean but never saw it.

She probably never imagined anything so big. All she had to do was look in the mirror and she'd see this blue. The ocean that lived in her eyes.

I stare at the ocean. And I think I see her, waiting for me. I call out to her. 'Momma? Can you hear me? Momma?'

(*No answer.*)

She doesn't answer back. That's one thing I learned about the ocean. It's so big. It's so blue. But it ain't much for conversation. Momma?

24

The Ladder Store.

JEFF and GEORGE are covered in blood. GEORGE has a drink.

GEORGE: (*As Mom.*) This reminds me of when your brother George was born.

There was so much blood. His umbilical cord was wrapped around his throat.

He couldn't breathe.

But they unwrapped it and he started to cry. My God what a set of lungs he had.

It was the single greatest sound I ever heard in my entire life.

JEFF: I can hold my breath for over eight minutes.

GEORGE: That's impossible.

JEFF: No, it's not.

I trained myself in the bathtub. Like Houdini.

Time me.

(*JEFF holds his breath.*)

GEORGE: Stop being ridiculous.

(*JEFF tries to look extra relaxed.*)

Cut it out, Jeffry.

(*She hits him in the back.*)

JEFF: Mom!

GEORGE: What?

Your shenanigans just about scared me half to death.

(*The POET wakes up.*)

JEFF: Do you know where you are?

POET: Have you ever seen the world without any pretense?
We're dying. All of us. We're all dying.

(*He cries.*)

JEFF: It worked.

GEORGE: I'm going out for a smoke.

JEFF: Mom, no cigarettes.

GEORGE: Jeffry, I just helped perform a heart transplant. I
deserve a cigarette.

(*He goes.*)

POET: That's your mother, isn't it?

JEFF: Yes.

She's not taking care of herself.

She's going to die again if she keeps this up.

POET: You love her so much, yet you hate her because she
loves your brother more.

JEFF: It's true.

POET: It's tragic. You have such a beautiful soul.

(*The POET cries.*)

JEFF: You can see my soul?

POET: Yes. It's so innocent.

JEFF: Does it have a color?

POET: It's blue. Like the sky.

JEFF: I love blue. It's my favorite color.

POET: If you would like I'll write a poem about your soul.

JEFF: Yes, please.

   (*The POET takes out paper and pen.*)

   No one's ever written anything about me. Let alone about my soul.

   (*JEFF poses, like for a portrait.*)

   Like this?

POET: That's fine.

   (*JEFF tries another pose.*)

JEFF: What about like this?

POET: Either way, it doesn't really matter.

JEFF: Like this.

   (*Another pose.*

   The MILLIONAIRE wakes up.)

MILLIONAIRE: What the fuck?

JEFF: How do you feel? A little nausea is normal.

MILLIONAIRE: It's gone, isn't it?

   I don't feel anything.

POET: I'm so sorry.

MILLIONAIRE: I gave all my money to a pimp, didn't I?

POET: You saw another person's needs and responded.

JEFF: Excuse me, he's writing a poem about my soul.

MILLIONAIRE: Shut up, Jeff!

   (*MILLIONAIRE takes out a cell-phone.*)

   It's me. I'm back. Yeah. I gave all my money to a pimp. Get it back. He's in Bermuda. Yeah. Take the plane. Bye.

   (*He hangs up.*)

   Don't give me that look.

   My blood and sweat are in that money. I can't just give it away.

POET: Will you listen to yourself?

MILLIONAIRE: I sound like I'm talking sense again.

POET: You used to see a different world. You saw a flower and talked about the inevitable decay of beauty. You saw the river and understood time.

MILLIONAIRE: Mid-life crisis bullshit. Why couldn't I just
buy a yacht like everybody else?

But no! I had to be different. That's what my mistress
always said. My mistress!

(*Cell-phone.*) It's me. I'm back. I was out of town on
business. Business! I'm sorry I didn't call. I'll get our suite
at the Plaza. Ten thirty. I hope you're feeling naughty.

(*He makes a cat-like growl into the phone and then a dog bark.
A horse whinny. He laughs. He realizes where he is.*)

I'll see you there.

(*He hangs up.*)

The shit that comes out of her mouth, I swear –

It would make a sailor blush.

Nice girl. Smart as a whip.

She's actually a Yale grad.

But most of the time when I'm with her I feel alone.

And when I'm alone, I wish I was dead.

I should cry now.

Fuck! I can't cry.

POET: We can go back under the bridge. By the river. You
love the river.

MILLIONAIRE: It's full of dirty needles and dead bodies.

POET: We'll get drunk and bay at the moon.

MILLIONAIRE: Fuck this.

I'm outta here.

I'm gonna sue both your asses. Expect to hear from my
attorney.

(*CUSTOMER enters. She's dressed like a lawyer.*)

CUSTOMER: I'll provide legal counsel pro bono.

JEFF: What's pro bono?

MILLIONAIRE: It means for free, dumbass.

(*MILLIONAIRE begins to leave in a huff.
GEORGE enters carrying Baked Alaska.*)

GEORGE: Are you leaving already?

MILLIONAIRE: Yeah.

I've got to get my money back and fuck my mistress and
say hi to my wife and my children.

GEORGE: Do you have children, too?

MILLIONAIRE: Yes, I do.

GEORGE: How old are your little buggers?

MILLIONAIRE: One is twelve and the other is fourteen.
Scratch that.
One is eleven and the other is fifteen.
No.
That's not right. Fuck.
Just a second.
(*He dials his phone.*)
Hey. How old are my children?
Really?
(*He hangs up his phone.*)
One is thirteen and the other is seventeen.

GEORGE: Those are wonderful ages. I can remember when
my son George was seventeen he was ranked second in the
state in the quarter mile and he also won highest honors at
the regional piano recital. Do you remember that, Jeff?

JEFF: I sure do.

MILLIONAIRE: Well, I better be going.

GEORGE: Do you want a little snack for the road? Take this
Baked Alaska.

MILLIONAIRE: Are you sure?

GEORGE: I insist.

MILLIONAIRE: Thank you.
I love Baked Alaska.

GEORGE: Don't be a stranger, you hear?
(*The MILLIONAIRE leaves eating the Baked Alaska. We cannot
hear the MILLIONAIRE's reply because his mouth is full of
Baked Alaska.*)

MILLIONAIRE: I would try not to be a stranger, but who
isn't a stranger to everyone else. I remember reading 'The
Stranger' by Camus in college. It had such a profound

effect on me. But honestly, I thought of Camus more as an essayist rather than a novelist. To this day, I still believe that the existentialists are essentially correct. It is man's duty to create meaning from one moment to the next but most of the time I find that burden too great. And allow my life to become devoid of meaning.

GEORGE: (*Continues as MILLIONAIRE exits. Looking at CUSTOMER.*) Who are you? Who is this?

JEFF: Mom, this is our lawyer.

CUSTOMER: Nice to meet you.

GEORGE: Likewise. I've got game hen roasting in the oven. While we're waiting can I fix you a drink?

CUSTOMER: I don't see why not.

GEORGE: What about you, Mr Poet?

POET: No thank you. I get drunk on the world.

GEORGE: You might sing a different tune once you've tried my Martini.
(*GEORGE shakes some drinks in a cocktail shaker.*
Pours three Martinis. Gives one to the POET and one to the CUSTOMER.)
I'd like to propose a toast. To my son, Jeff.
However much he grows up, he'll always be my baby.
(*GEORGE slaps JEFF's butt.*)

ALL: To Jeff!
(*They clink glasses and drink. GEORGE chugs hers.*)

CUSTOMER: I'd better get started on the paperwork.

JEFF: The files are in back. Let me show you.

CUSTOMER: Thank you for the drink. You make a very good Martini.

GEORGE: I'm glad somebody appreciates me around here.

JEFF: I appreciate you, Mom.

GEORGE: Do you really, Jeffrey?
Ask yourself that.

JEFF: (*He asks himself.*) Do I appreciate Mom?
(*He thinks.*)

(*He answers himself.*) Yes, I do.

(*To GEORGE.*) Yes, Mom. I do appreciate you.

GEORGE: I'm happy to hear that.

CUSTOMER: Where are those files you were talking about?

JEFF: Follow me.

(*JEFF leads the CUSTOMER into the back.*)

POET: I should get going, too.

GEORGE: Are you sure? We've only just gotten acquainted
    and you haven't tasted my game hen.

POET: I want to rediscover the world.

I hope you and Jeff can forgive each other and love each
    other unconditionally.

GEORGE: I don't believe unconditional love can exist in this
    world.

POET: Of course it exists.

You just can't expect love's reciprocation.

GEORGE: I suppose you're right, Mr Poet.

But I find when I love something too hard and then it
    slips away my heart breaks and I am absolutely torn to
    smithereens.

POET: That's what the heart is meant to do.

GEORGE: What?

POET: Break.

(*JEFF enters.*)

JEFF: I'm back!

POET: Goodbye.

Thank you, Jeff.

JEFF: My pleasure.

I'm glad we got your heart back where it truly belongs.

POET: Me too.

GEORGE: Bon voyage!

(*The POET goes.*)

JEFF: Why did you say 'bon voyage'?

Is he going on a cruise or something?

GEORGE: No, he's not going on a cruise.

But I hate saying goodbye.

And 'bon voyage' sounds so much more beautiful.

JEFF: What's it mean?

GEORGE: It's French. It means, literally, 'good voyage'.

JEFF: 'Bon voyage'. I'll have to remember that one.

GEORGE: Are you hungry, Jeff?

JEFF: I guess I could eat.

GEORGE: I'll go check on the game hen.

I'll be right back, baby.

(*She kisses him flush on the lips and goes.*

He wipes it off.)

JEFF: Yuck.

25

The beach. Bermuda.

The HOOKER comes on with a suitcase.

She takes off all of the jewelry and gives it to T-BONE.

T-BONE: What are you doing?

HOOKER: I'm leaving, T-Bone.

T-BONE: Where are you going?

HOOKER: I don't like it here.

T-BONE: What's not to like?

Pink sand. Blue water.

Sunsets that melt and bleed.

HOOKER: I hate swimming.

I hate tanning.

This isn't real life, T-Bone. I want real life again.

I wanna go home.

T-BONE: Fine, baby.

We'll go home.

HOOKER: I don't want you to come.

T-BONE: Baby, look what I bought you.

HOOKER: I don't want any more presents.

(*Gets on one knee and takes out a wedding ring.*)

T-BONE: Baby, will you marry me?

(*Silence.*)

This is where you say yes and we live happily ever after.

HOOKER: I can't, T-Bone.

T-BONE: Sure you can. It's just three letters. Y-E-S. Yes.

(*The WAITER enters with another suitcase.*)

WAITER: She's with me, Mr Bone.

T-BONE: Is that true, baby?

HOOKER: It's true.

WAITER: Did you give me my cut from your appointment with the Asian tourists?

HOOKER: I gave it to you already.

WAITER: Bitch, don't make me smack you.

HOOKER: I gave you most of it. (*She gives the WAITER the money.*) I wanted to buy a fashion magazine for the plane.

WAITER: Baby, you give me that money and I'll buy you the fashion magazine.

HOOKER: I'm sorry, baby.

(*He hits her in the face.*)

T-BONE: Don't hit her!

WAITER: Stay outta this, Mr Bone.

HOOKER: You better listen to this motherfucker, T-Bone. Stay out of this.

T-BONE: Okay, I'll stay out of this.

WAITER: I'm sorry, baby. But I can't have you stealing from me.

I love you. It hurts me so much when I hit you. You know that, don't you?

HOOKER: I know.

WAITER: I'm sorry you made me hit you.

HOOKER: No. I'm sorry.

WAITER: Gimme a kiss and take my bags to the taxi.

(*She kisses him and carries both suitcases. They're heavy.*)

HOOKER: Bye, T-Bone.

T-BONE: Bye, baby.

HOOKER: I hope you enjoy Bermuda.

Send me a postcard sometime.

(*She goes.*)

T-BONE: So that's the way it's gonna be?

WAITER: That's the way it's gonna be.

She didn't want to lie on the beach sipping umbrella drinks.

She's a people person.

She wants to work.

You didn't listen.

T-BONE: I gave her what everybody wants.

WAITER: Not everybody, T-Bone.

(*The WAITER bows and leaves.*)

T-BONE: No, not everybody.

(*T-BONE is alone. He watches the surf.*)

26

The Ladder Store.
JEFF tends the ladders.
GEORGE enters and turns out the light.
JEFF goes into a fighting position.

GEORGE: (*As Mom.*) You thought I forgot, didn't you?

JEFF: Forgot what?

(*GEORGE takes out a little cupcake with a lit candle in it.*)

GEORGE: Happy birthday.

JEFF: Thanks, Mom.

GEORGE: I would have thrown you a big party but I know you hate parties.

JEFF: Thanks for respecting my needs, Mom.

GEORGE: So I decided to throw you just a teensy-weensy party. Come in, Miss Lawyer-woman!

JEFF: Mom!

(*The CUSTOMER enters from the back in a birthday hat.*)

GEORGE / CUSTOMER: (*Singing.*)

Happy birthday to you

Happy birthday to you

Happy birthday dear Jeff

Happy birthday to you.

GEORGE: (*Not singing.*) Make a wish.

(*JEFF considers a couple of different wishes.*

And then finally decides on one.

He takes a big breath, much bigger than necessary for one little candle.)

Just a sec.

(*GEORGE lights a cigarette from the candle on JEFF's cupcake.*

JEFF blows out the candle.)

CUSTOMER: I hope your wish comes true.

JEFF: Thank you.

CUSTOMER: I have to run. I've got a court date.

Happy birthday.

JEFF: You too.

CUSTOMER: It's not my birthday.

JEFF: Sorry.

I said 'you too' out of reflex. Don't you hate that?

CUSTOMER: I do.

Goodbye.

(*The CUSTOMER leaves.*)

GEORGE: What did you wish for?

JEFF: I wished that you tell me the story of the day I was born.

GEORGE: That was a trick question.

You're not supposed to tell anybody your wish because now it won't come true.

JEFF: Mom! That's not fair!

GEORGE: I was just kidding. It's really not much of a story.

JEFF: I'll start: You woke up at two AM.

GEORGE: I woke up at two AM and said to your father:

JEFF: 'This is it.'

GEORGE: Who's telling this story?

JEFF: You are.

GEORGE: I said to your father 'This is it,' so we went to the hospital.

The doctor came in and your father was sleeping in the bed and I was sitting in the chair.

You weren't ready to come out yet. The doctor said: 'Come back in ten days.'

JEFF: (*Corrects her.*) Hours.

(*JEFF mouths some of the words because he knows the story and it's his favorite story in the whole world.*)

GEORGE: Come back in ten hours. So we went home. We slept. We came back in ten hours, and you came out.

JEFF: Just like that.

GEORGE: Just like that.

JEFF: Thanks for giving birth to me, Mom.

GEORGE: Don't mention it. Can your mother have a hug for giving birth to you?

JEFF: Yes, ma'am.

(*JEFF hugs GEORGE. GEORGE doesn't let go.*)

27

In the street.
The HOOKER is working. She's got a black eye.
The POET walks by.

HOOKER: Hey, honey. You looking for a party? You look lonely.

POET: It's me.

HOOKER: Me who? Is this a game? I love playing games, honey.

POET: I'm the poet. You gave me a pro bono blowjob.

HOOKER: You're gonna have to give me a little more.

POET: You washed my hair. We got beat up by T-Bone. We kidnapped the millionaire with my heart and he gave you ten million dollars.

HOOKER: Oh hey. How you doing?

POET: I'm well. How are you doing?

HOOKER: Aces. Business is booming.

(*The WAITER, in pimp clothes, opens the door.*)

WAITER: It's forty dollars for half an hour. You can do anything you want. You can even hit her. But no closed fist. What's our mantra baby?

WAITER / HOOKER: Black & Blue is bad for business.

HOOKER: Baby, this isn't a customer. This is an old friend.

WAITER: Can I get you a drink? Stawberry daiquiri? Pina Colada?

POET: No thanks, I get drunk on the world.

WAITER: Very good, sir.

(*He bows and closes the door.*)

POET: They can hit you now?

HOOKER: It's good for business. Lots of angry people in the world.

POET: Where's T-Bone?

HOOKER: He killed himself.

POET: He killed himself?

HOOKER: Yeah. In Bermuda.

I got word a few days ago.

POET: Does anybody know why?

HOOKER: It was his birthday. He always hated his birthday.

POET: I remember.

HOOKER: Hey! You got your heart back, didn't you?

POET: I did.

HOOKER: How's that going for you?

POET: Wonderful.

I can feel the world again. I can feel pain and joy.

HOOKER: Me? I couldn't work if I had that kind of heart.

POET: But it's the greatest gift God gave us. To feel.

HOOKER: I'm sure it's great. But I gotta make a living, you
know? To do the work I do you gotta be numb.

(*WAITER pops his head out.*)

WAITER: Excuse me. But I thought since this is a friend, you
might want a picture.

(*HOOKER and POET pose for picture.*)

POET: Aren't we supposed to say cheese?

HOOKER: No, we don't say anything out of respect for the
dead.

POET: Oh. Okay.

(*They don't say anything, the WAITER takes a picture.*)

WAITER: No big hurry, baby, but it's time for my bath.

HOOKER: Okay. Go inside and run the water.

POET: Nice meeting you.

WAITER: You too. Any friend of hers is a friend of mine.

(*He bows and goes back in.*)

HOOKER: I gotta go.

It was great seeing you again.

POET: You too.

HOOKER: If you're ever horny, drop by. I'll keep you on the
pro bono list. You can hit me if you want to.

But no closed fists! Black & Blue is bad for business.

POET: Take care of yourself.

HOOKER: You don't gotta worry about me, honey.

Taking care of me is my specialty.

(*She goes.*

The POET does too.)

28

JEFF and GEORGE.
GEORGE has a couple more drinks.

GEORGE: To tell you the truth if I had it all over again, I
wouldn't have any children.

JEFF: Don't say that, Mom.

GEORGE: I can say whatever I like.

JEFF: Watch your ash, Mom.

GEORGE: Don't tell me to watch my ass.

JEFF: Your ash.

Your ash.

(*Ash from the cigarette falls on GEORGE.*)

GEORGE: Goddamnit

JEFF: I told you to watch it.

GEORGE: Now my blouse is gonna have a hole in it.

JEFF: Let me take your drink for you.

GEORGE: Oh no.

I know what you're trying to do.

JEFF: I'm not doing anything.

GEORGE: Yes you are. I'm on to you, buster.

JEFF: Aren't you tired? Maybe you should take a nap, Mom.

GEORGE: You're just like your father. All you want to do is
shut me up. Well I'm not shutting up.

Get me another cigarette.

JEFF: There's none left.

GEORGE: Oh no you don't!

(*GEORGE looks in the pack. No more cigarettes.*)

What did you do with all my cigarettes?

JEFF: I didn't do anything.

You must have smoked them all.

GEORGE: That's ridiculous.

JEFF: It isn't ridiculous. You've been chain smoking like it's
your job.

GEORGE: Never mind.

I have a whole carton behind that ladder. Be a good boy
and get your mother the carton.

JEFF: Mom. You've had enough.

GEORGE: Jeffry! I do not want to fight about this.

(*JEFF gets the carton of cigarettes.
Gives her a pack.*)

*GEORGE taps it into a her hand like smokers do. Takes one out
and puts it in her mouth.)*

You got a light?

(*JEFF lights her cigarette.*)

Thank you, baby.

You'll always be my baby boy, Jeff.

That's why God made you the way he did. So you'd never
grow up and leave me like your brother.

JEFF: Don't talk that way about George.

GEORGE: You love a child for eighteen years. You pour
everything you have into him. And then: Poof! Gone. Not
even a puff of smoke.

JEFF: George loved you, Mom.

GEORGE: He didn't come back when I was in the hospital.

I bet you he didn't even come back for my funeral.

JEFF: Yes he did, Mom.

He was right up front and cried more than anybody.

GEORGE: He cried more than anybody?

JEFF: And then he took care of me, Mom.

He took such great care of me. He opened The Ladder
Store and sold hearts on the black market.

We always had enough food on the table and for ice cream
and for Ms Pac Man.

GEORGE: You love him, don't you?

JEFF: I do.

I love him very much.

GEORGE: I poured all my love into that boy.

Where did it all go? Have you ever asked yourself that?

Where did all of my love go?

JEFF: (*Asking himself.*) Where did all of Mom's love go?

(*GEORGE is hit with a pain in his chest.*)

GEORGE: Uh oh.

JEFF: What is it, Momma?

GEORGE: I think I'm having another heart attack.

(*She falls to the ground.*)

JEFF: I'll call for help.

GEORGE: No, baby.

   It's my time. Let me go.

JEFF: I'll put another heart in.

   I'll fix you right up.

   (*JEFF begins to go.*)

GEORGE: Jeffrey!

   (*JEFF stops.*)

JEFF: I'll ask myself again, where did all of Mom's love go?

GEORGE: There's no time. Say goodbye to your mother.

JEFF: No.

GEORGE: Then say bon voyage.

JEFF: No, ma'am.

GEORGE: Say it!

JEFF: Bon voyage.

GEORGE: I'll wait for you and your brother in heaven.

JEFF: That wasn't enough time!

   It's not fair.

GEORGE: Life isn't fair, Jeffery.

   You never could figure that out, could you?

   (*GEORGE dies.*

   JEFF cradles the body.)

29

Bermuda. The beach.

T-BONE holds the suitcase of money. He's wearing all of the gaudy jewelry from before, including the diamond tiara.

T-BONE: Dear, Momma.

   It's my birthday again. It's the day you died, too, giving
   birth to me. I'm rich, Momma. I got all the money I could
   ever want. But I'm so lonely. I lost the love of my life,
   Momma. I didn't listen to her. I couldn't hear what her
   heart needed.

I know about your heart, Momma. I know how strong it was. I know how brave you were. You wanted me to live instead of you. And I love you, Momma, but I think you made the wrong choice.

You shoulda chosen you, Momma. You shoulda chosen you.

(*He walks into the surf singing the first verse of 'Baby Mine'. The company sing the second verse with him.*)

30

The Ladder Store.
JEFF has a huge ladder that extends past the top of the stage. We can't see the top.
He's testing out the bottom. Trying the first few steps.
The POET enters.

JEFF: (*As GEORGE.*) Welcome to The Ladder Store. My name is George. Is there anything I can help you with?

POET: Hi, Jeff.

JEFF: I'm George. My brother Jeff put my heart into his body. Are you looking for any particular ladder today?

POET: I'm actually looking for a ladder to heaven, George.

JEFF: This is a ladder to heaven.

Jeff kept talking about it, so I built one.

POET: That's so touching.

JEFF: I was just about to test it out, but I didn't have anyone to hold the bottom.

POET: I'll hold it.

JEFF: You will?

POET: Of course.

JEFF: And will you hold onto this cooler?

POET: Sure. What's in it?

JEFF: My brother Jeff's heart. So don't put any beers in it or anything.

POET: I won't.

(*JEFF begins to climb the ladder.*)

JEFF: Is there anybody you want me to say hi to?

I'm going to say hi to our Mom, a couple of Jeff's dead pets, and Vince Lombardi.

POET: Say hi to T-Bone for me. And The Millionaire

JEFF: T-Bone and The Millionaire? No problem.

POET: I'll see you when you get back.

JEFF: Will you say 'bon voyage' to me?

POET: Sure. Bon voyage.

JEFF: You too.

POET: I'm not going anywhere.

JEFF: I know. I hate it when I do that.

(*JEFF climbs the ladder up out of sight.
The POET holds the bottom.*)

POET: This is the poem I wrote about Jeff's soul:

I hate it when people make excuses about their work, but this is my first poem since I got my heart back so please be a little kind.

Ahem.

There once was a man from Hyannis.

Just kidding.

I went looking for the perfect image of blue
Yes, there's snow in afternoon shadow,
Yes, wind against cut glass,
And yes, of course, the still cold light of stars
But I know these images are far from perfect
My rummaging ends in failure.
Even though my voice has never felt so clear
It fails me.
I watch the blue blood slide back slowly
towards my heart.
And then, yes, I remember:
my mother's eyes.
That's the final image of this poem and this play:

The blue I saw in my mother's eyes.

That and Jeff with George's heart in his body climbing the ladder to heaven.

(*POET looks up at JEFF on ladder.*)

END OF PLAY

MR MARMALADE

Characters

LUCY, 4 years old. Has a vivid imagination.

MR MARMALADE, her imaginary friend. Dresses nice. Never has any time for her.

SOOKIE, Lucy's Mom. Relies on men for more than they're good for.

EMILY, the babysitter. The first girl in her class to get boobs.

GEORGE, her boyfriend. A jock. Wears a leather jacket.

LARRY, 5 years old. Has bandages on his wrists. The youngest suicide attempt in the history of New Jersey.

BRADLEY, Mr Marmalade's personal assistant. Can sing like an angel.

CACTUS and SUNFLOWER, talking plants.

MAN, a one-night stand.

Mr Marmalade was first performed on 25 April 2004 by South Coast Repertory in Costa Mesa, California, with the following company:

LUCY, Eliza Pryor Nagel
MR MARMALADE, Glenn Fleshier
SOOKIE / SUNFLOWER / EMILY, Heidi Dippold
GEORGE / CACTUS / MAN, Larry Bates
LARRY, Guilford Adams
BRADLEY, Marc Vietor

Directed by Ethan McSweeny
Set design by Rachel Hauck
Costume design by Angela Baloh Calin
Lighting design by Scott Zielinkski
Sound design by Michael Roth
Assistant Director Joshua N Hsu
Dramaturg Jerry Patch
Production Manager Tom Aberger
Stage Manager Jamie A Tucker

1

OF THE STRAINED RELATIONSHIP OF LUCY AND HER IMAGINARY
FRIEND MR MARMALADE

*A living room in New Jersey. Let's not get very naturalistic about it. More
the suggestion of a room than a room.*
*LUCY is playing with Ken and Barbie. She wears a pink tutu in a state
of disrepair. Barbie wears a tutu too.*
*MR MARMALADE appears. He's very well dressed. Suit, briefcase, nice
shoes.*

MR MARMALADE: Good evening.

LUCY: I thought you weren't coming.

MR MARMALADE: I carved out some time.

LUCY: Thirty minutes?

MR MARMALADE: Ten.

LUCY: That's not very many.

MR MARMALADE: It's the best I could do. Next week will be
better. I promise.

LUCY: We'd better get started.

MR MARMALADE: What is it today?

LUCY: House.

MR MARMALADE: I see.

(*He opens his briefcase and whips out a tea set. Cups, saucers,
spoons.*)

Whenever you're ready.

LUCY: Come down here.

(*He sits.*)

Would you like a cup of coffee?

MR MARMALADE: Have we started?

LUCY: Yes.

MR MARMALADE: I would love a cup of coffee.

(*She pours coffee.*)

LUCY: How do you take it?

MR MARMALADE: Black.

(*She puts sugar in the coffee. Gives him the cup.*)

I said black.

LUCY: Did you? I'm sorry.

Would you like another cup?

MR MARMALADE: Yes, please.

LUCY: Oh shoot, we just ran out. Would you like me to brew some more?

MR MARMALADE: Don't worry about it.

LUCY: Are you sure?

MR MARMALADE: Are you angry with me, Lucy?

LUCY: Why would I be angry with you, honey?

MR MARMALADE: Not play angry. Real angry.

LUCY: I'm not angry.

I just wish you weren't so busy.

MR MARMALADE: So do I. I wish I could play with you all night, but work is crazy right now.

LUCY: I know. I'm sorry.

We'd better keep going.

Not much time.

MR MARMALADE: Okay.

LUCY: Would you like more coffee?

MR MARMALADE: I thought we ran out.

LUCY: I have a fresh pot right here.

Black?

MR MARMALADE: Please.

(*She pours some coffee.*

He sips it.)

LUCY: What do you think?

MR MARMALADE: Delicious.

LUCY: It's a new blend I had flown in from Peru.

MR MARMALADE: It's absolutely wonderful, Lucy.

LUCY: I'm so glad you're home from work. You have no idea how lonely this house gets.

MR MARMALADE: I can only imagine.

It's so good to be home.

LUCY: Why don't you touch me anymore?

SOOKIE: (*Off.*) Lucy!!

MR MARMALADE: What?

LUCY: You haven't touched me in weeks.

Is there somebody else?

MR MARMALADE: What?

No. Don't be ridiculous.

LUCY: Someone at work? That new intern?

SOOKIE: (*Off.*) Lucy!? What are you doing, Lucy?

LUCY: I'm busy (*To MR MARMALADE.*) Is there somebody else?

MR MARMALADE: Of course not. How could you ask me such a thing?

LUCY: You're at the office until the dead of night. And when you are home you barely even look at me, let alone lay a finger on me.

MR MARMALADE: I'm tired when I get home. I'm exhausted. All I can think of is going to sleep.

I barely have the energy to shovel food in my mouth.

LUCY: Excuses, excuses.

MR MARMALADE: I'm sorry.

I'll do better.

Cut back at work.

We'll take a vacation. Mexico. Cabo San Lucas. First class across the board.

LUCY: Mexico!

You promise?

MR MARMALADE: I promise.

(*SOOKIE enters in a slip and high heels. She carries two dresses.*)

SOOKIE: Which one?

LUCY: Mom, I'm busy.

SOOKIE: What are you doing?

LUCY: Mr Marmalade just got home from the office and he has to leave in like five minutes so I'd greatly appreciate it if you left us alone.

SOOKIE: Hello, Mr Marmalade.

MR MARMALADE: Hello, Mother.

LUCY: He says hello.

SOOKIE: Tell him hello for me too.

MR MARMALADE: Such a nice woman your mother.

SOOKIE: Which dress should I wear?

LUCY: I think it's very rude for you to barge in here when I
    have company. You owe Mr Marmalade an apology. You
    know how precious his time is.

SOOKIE: Mr Marmalade, I'm very sorry.

MR MARMALADE: It's not a problem at all. I adore the time I
    spend with your mother.

LUCY: He accepts your apology. Begrudgingly, I might add.

SOOKIE: Maybe Mr Marmalade has a preference about which
    dress I wear.

MR MARMALADE: I prefer the red dress, although I imagine
    just about anything would look stunning on you.

LUCY: He likes the red one.

SOOKIE: Me too. Thank you, Mr Marmalade.

    (*She kisses LUCY on the head and exits.*)

MR MARMALADE: There's no need to thank me. I'm flattered
    that she holds my opinion in such high regard.

LUCY: Where were we?

MR MARMALADE: Mexico.

LUCY: That's right. Cabo San Lucas.

MR MARMALADE: First class across the board.

    A huge white bed with pillows stuffed with ostrich feathers.

    Men in white tuxedos holding umbrellas for the sun.

    Top-shelf margaritas on the hotel veranda watching the
    sunset.

LUCY: When can we go?

MR MARMALADE: We'll go next month.

    Work will lighten up.

LUCY: You promise you're not cheating on me?

MR MARMALADE: I promise I'm not cheating on you.

LUCY: You pinky swear?

MR MARMALADE: I pinky swear.

(*They pinky swear.*)

LUCY: I knew you weren't. Oh, honey, I'm sorry I accused you of that.

I'm alone here all by myself night and day.

My imagination runs wild.

You have no idea.

(*His beeper goes off. It startles him.*)

MR MARMALADE: Oh shit, my beeper.

LUCY: You're not going to go back to the office tonight, are you, dear?

MR MARMALADE: Not play beeper. My real beeper.

LUCY: No

MR MARMALADE: I have to go.

LUCY: You said ten minutes.

MR MARMALADE: I know I did. But I have to go.

LUCY: When will I see you again?

MR MARMALADE: Let me check my palm.

(*Scrolls through his palm pilot.*)

This week is terrible. I might have forty-five minutes on Thursday. Maybe we could do sushi. I'll have Bradley call you.

LUCY: You said we'd do sushi last week.

MR MARMALADE: I know I did. I'm sorry.

(*Kisses her on the head.*)

I have to go. Goodbye.

(*He disappears.*)

LUCY: Goodbye.

(*SOOKIE enters in the red dress.*)

SOOKIE: What do you think?

(*She sashays.*)

LUCY: It's okay.

SOOKIE: What do you think, Mr Marmalade?

LUCY: He's not here.

SOOKIE: Where is he?

LUCY: At the office.

He's a very important man. I can't expect him to spend his whole night here drinking coffee with me.

SOOKIE: Babysitter'll be here in half an hour.

Can you hold down the fort until then?

LUCY: Which one is it?

SOOKIE: Emily.

LUCY: Ugggh.

SOOKIE: You like Emily.

LUCY: No I don't. She smells like cigarettes.

She only talks about her boyfriend and her breasts coming in.

SOOKIE: Emily is a very nice girl and you're going to have a good time.

LUCY: I don't see the point of having a babysitter at all.

SOOKIE: Lucy, you're four years old.

LUCY: I can take care of myself.

SOOKIE: You're too young to take care of yourself.

LUCY: Who says?

SOOKIE: I say.

(*The doorbell rings.*)

We'll have to discuss this later.

How do I look?

LUCY: Fine.

SOOKIE: Just fine or pretty good?

LUCY: Just fine.

SOOKIE: Thank you for your support, Lucy.

(*Kisses her on the head.*)

No TV and in bed by nine o'clock. Do you hear me?

LUCY: Yes, ma'am.

SOOKIE: Goodnight, dear.

(*She goes.*)

LUCY: Goodnight.

(*LUCY is alone.*)

2

OF THE CONVERSATION BETWEEN LUCY AND EMILY THE
BABYSITTER, DURING WHICH THEY TALK ABOUT MR MARMALADE
AND HIS DELINQUENT BEHAVIOR AND HOW MEN ARE LIKE THAT
IN GENERAL UNLESS YOU KEEP THEM IN LINE

*EMILY watches TV, eating a big bowl of popcorn. LUCY is onstage
talking into a hairbrush like it's a cell-phone.*

LUCY: (*On phone.*) You're breaking up.

No, I can hear you now.

Tonight?

Nothing. Just hanging out. I've got a babysitter.

I know, can you believe it?

No. She's okay.

Kinda dumb.

She smokes cigarettes. Her clothes smell like cigarettes.

I know, disgusting, right?

Teenagers.

It's an awkward time, you're right.

She's got a boyfriend. Yeah. I don't know, I'll ask her.

(*To EMILY.*) Have you had sex with your boyfriend yet?

EMILY: What?

LUCY: (*On phone.*) She's totally avoiding the question.

Yeah. I bet she has, too.

She doesn't look like a virgin.

EMILY: Who are you talking to?

LUCY: (*On the phone.*) Just a sec.

(*To EMILY.*) I'm on the phone. Would you mind not
interrupting? Thanks.

(*On the phone.*) She keeps interrupting.

I know? Right?

Mind your manners. I will tell her that.

You gotta go?

Are you sure?

Okay. No. I understand.

Ciao.

(*Hangs up the phone.*)

EMILY: Who were you talking to?

LUCY: No one you know.

EMILY: Was it Mr Marmalade?

LUCY: How do you know Mr Marmalade?

EMILY: We hang out all the time.

LUCY: You do not.

EMILY: We go to the mall and get manicures.

LUCY: Mr Marmalade does not get manicures!

EMILY: Chill out. We don't go to the mall.

Your Mom told me about him.

LUCY: What'd she say?

EMILY: Says he's a deadbeat.

LUCY: He's very busy.

He's a very important man.

EMILY: Don't matter how important he is. He's gotta make time for you.

LUCY: He wants to make more time for me.

Things are just so crazy at the office right now.

EMILY: My boyfriend George used to say he was too busy to hang out with me.

LUCY: What'd you do?

EMILY: I stopped hooking up with him.

LUCY: Then did he have more time for you?

EMILY: You better believe he did.

LUCY: That's what I'll do.

EMILY: Do you even hook up with Mr Marmalade?

LUCY: I think I do.

EMILY: Either you do or you don't.

LUCY: Then I do.

EMILY: Let me talk to him.

LUCY: He's in a meeting.

EMILY: Gimme the phone.

LUCY: No.

EMILY: Fine. I've got my own phone.

(*She dials her real cell-phone.*)

LUCY: You don't even know his number.

EMILY: Hello? Mr Marmalade?

It's Emily. Hey, what's up?

LUCY: You're not talking to him.

EMILY: No, she's right here. I know, she gets pretty annoying, doesn't she?

LUCY: That's not him.

EMILY: She totally has a crush on you.

(*LUCY is grabbing for the phone.*)

LUCY: Shut up I do not!

EMILY: She wants to marry you and have your babies!

LUCY: I do not!

(*LUCY grabs the cell-phone.*)

Hello? Mr Marmalade? Mr Marmalade?

EMILY: He must have hung up.

LUCY: You weren't talking to him.

EMILY: I totally was.

LUCY: NO YOU WEREN'T!

EMILY: Okay. Chill out.

I wasn't talking to Mr Marmalade. Jesus.

LUCY: You don't even know him.

EMILY: I've never met him, okay?

LUCY: Okay.

EMILY: Jealousy is not attractive to men, Lucy.

Trust me.

(*Silence.*)

LUCY: Let's play Tea Party.

EMILY: I want to watch TV.

LUCY: I want to play Tea Party.

EMILY: My show's on.

LUCY: It's on commercial.

EMILY: So I'm watching the commercial.

LUCY: What do you think my Mom is paying you for?

  I want a Tea Party.

EMILY: All right, all right.

LUCY: Come down here.

  (*She sits on the ground.*)

  What kind of tea would you like?

EMILY: What kind do you have?

LUCY: Earl Grey, English Breakfast, Green Tea, Darjeeling Oolong.

EMILY: I don't know.

  Which one is good?

LUCY: I prefer Darjeeling Oolong.

EMILY: I'll have the English Breakfast.

LUCY: Which is also excellent.

  (*She pours imaginary water. Puts in an imaginary tea bag.*)

  How would you like it?

  I take mine with sugar and milk.

EMILY: That sounds pretty good.

LUCY: Wonderful.

  (*She adds sugar and milk.*

  Hands it to EMILY, who tentatively sips.)

  Well?

EMILY: It's good.

LUCY: Not too sweet?

EMILY: No, it's really good.

  (*EMILY chugs the rest of her imaginary tea.*)

  Listen, I'm gonna go outside for a few minutes.

LUCY: But it's a tea party.

EMILY: I finished my tea.

LUCY: But I made cucumber sandwiches.

EMILY: I'm sorry.

  I'm not very good at make-believe.

LUCY: You're going to smoke a cigarette.

EMILY: I like a cigarette after a cup of tea.

  Why don't you invite Mr Marmalade to your tea party?

LUCY: He's busy.

EMILY: I'll be back in a few minutes, okay?

LUCY: Fine.

(*EMILY leaves.*

BRADLEY appears, unseen by LUCY.

He's dressed exactly like MR MARMALADE. Nice suit. Shoes.

Briefcase. He also wears big wrap around sunglasses.)

BRADLEY: Lucy.

LUCY: Oh, you scared me, Bradley.

BRADLEY: Sorry.

(*They kiss on the cheek. Very adult-like.*)

LUCY: What are you doing here? I wasn't expecting to hear
from you until the first of the week.

BRADLEY: The schedule has changed. Mr M was hoping you
would be free this weekend.

LUCY: I'm free.

BRADLEY: Excellent. I'll pencil you in for brunch on Sunday.

LUCY: I was just sitting down for tea, would you like some?

BRADLEY: That would be delightful.

Do you happen to have Darjeeling Oolong?

LUCY: Of course.

(*BRADLEY sits. She pours the tea.*)

I'm afraid I'm fresh out of milk.

BRADLEY: No problem. I've got some.

(*He opens his briefcase and takes out some milk.*

He pours it.)

LUCY: Thank you, Bradley.

BRADLEY: Are those cucumber sandwiches?

LUCY: Would you like one?

BRADLEY: Yes, please.

(*He takes one. Eats.*)

Nothing complements a cup of tea like a cucumber
sandwich.

LUCY: I know what you mean.

BRADLEY: What time would be convenient for you on
Sunday?

LUCY: Any time would be fine.

Why are you wearing sunglasses?

BRADLEY: Because UV rays are bad for your eyes.

Haven't you heard?

LUCY: It's dark out, Bradley.

BRADLEY: What time on Sunday?

LUCY: Noon.

BRADLEY: (*Writing.*) Sunday. Noon. Brunch with Lucy. Got it.
Thank you for the tea and the cucumber sandwich, but I'd
better get back to the office.

(*She grabs BRADLEY's sunglasses. BRADLEY's got a big fat
shiner under his right eye.*)

LUCY: Oh my God.

BRADLEY: It's nothing.

LUCY: Did he do this?

BRADLEY: I fell down some stairs.

LUCY: Bradley, did Mr Marmalade hit you?

BRADLEY: It was an accident. He didn't really mean to hit
me.

LUCY: Why did he hit you?

BRADLEY: It was my fault.

I forgot to pick up his dry cleaning, when I knew he had a
very important dinner with a client. I knew he needed his
gray suit. I forgot to pick it up. It was all my fault.

LUCY: He hit you over the dry cleaning.

BRADLEY: He's under so much pressure. You have no idea.

LUCY: That's no excuse.

BRADLEY: You're not going to tell anyone, are you?

LUCY: I think I should.

BRADLEY: No! You have to promise me you won't.

Lucy, I can't lose this job.

LUCY: There are things more important than your job,
Bradley.

BRADLEY: Please, Lucy. I'm begging you. Please don't tell anyone.

LUCY: I won't. But it's against my better judgement, Bradley.

BRADLEY: Thank you, Lucy.

LUCY: But if anything else happens to you, if he touches one hair on your head I'm calling the police.

BRADLEY: It won't happen again.

Things are going to calm down. He won't be so stressed.

LUCY: Give me a hug, Bradley.

(*BRADLEY hugs LUCY.*)

BRADLEY: Well, gotta get back to work.

(*He puts on his sunglasses.*)

You're on for brunch on Sunday at noon.

LUCY: Take care of yourself, Bradley.

BRADLEY: I will.

LUCY: Bradley?

BRADLEY: Yes.

LUCY: Did Mr M mention anything about Mexico?

Plane tickets?

Hotel reservations?

BRADLEY: Not a thing.

LUCY: Oh.

BRADLEY: But sometimes he makes very important reservations himself.

LUCY: I'm sure he's already taken care of it.

(*EMILY enters. Doesn't see BRADLEY.*)

EMILY: Did Mr Marmalade come for the tea party?

LUCY: No. It was his personal assistant. Bradley.

EMILY: He sent his assistant?

BRADLEY: This is your babysitter? How grim.

LUCY: Mr Marmalade was too busy to come himself. He's under a tremendous amount of pressure at work.

EMILY: What's Bradley like? Is he cute?

BRADLEY: I look awful!

You should have seen me ten years ago.

LUCY: I'm worried about him.

Bradley doesn't take care of himself.

BRADLEY: Maybe not like in the old days, but I try to stay fit.

EMILY: What do you mean he doesn't take care of himself?

How can an imaginary personal assistant not take care of himself?

LUCY: He doesn't have much self-esteem.

He gets pushed around.

BRADLEY: That's not fair, Lucy. That's only half the story.

EMILY: Sounds to me like he should get a new boss and you should get a new friend.

LUCY: Things are going to lighten up at work soon.

And then Bradley won't have to sacrifice himself the way he does all the time.

BRADLEY: Thank you, Lucy.

Goodbye.

(*He disappears.*)

EMILY: When I was your age I liked to play line.

LUCY: How do you play line?

EMILY: You just get in a line and pretend to be waiting for something.

I liked to wait for the bus.

LUCY: That doesn't sound very fun.

EMILY: Do you want to try it?

LUCY: I guess so.

EMILY: Here, you get behind me.

(*They stand in a line.*)

What are you waiting for?

LUCY: The butcher.

EMILY: No. We're at the bus station.

What bus are you waiting for?

LUCY: The number seven.

EMILY: There is no bus number seven, Lucy.

LUCY: Then I guess it's going to be a long wait.

EMILY: You can't even play line right.

(*The doorbell rings.*)

LUCY: Who is that?

EMILY: It's George, my boyfriend.

LUCY: George isn't supposed to come over.

EMILY: He's already over.

LUCY: You two are going to have sex!

EMILY: We're going to do our math homework.

(*She puts on lipstick and fusses with her hair.*)

How do I look?

LUCY: Easy.

EMILY: Good.

(*She tugs at her breasts, trying to make them look bigger. The doorbell rings again.*)

Coming. I'm coming!

(*Opens the door. GEORGE bounds in.*)

GEORGE: Hello, beautiful.

(*GEORGE gives her a big kiss. Bends her backwards. Grabs her breasts.*)

EMILY: George!

GEORGE: Shut up, you love it.

EMILY: The kid.

GEORGE: Oh shit. Hiya, kid. Lucy, right?

(*LUCY doesn't say anything.*)

I got a surprise for you, Lucy. (*Calling.*) Larry!

EMILY: You brought Larry?

GEORGE: My folks are out playing bridge. I have to watch the stupid fucker. (*Calling.*) Larry!

(*Sheepishly LARRY enters. He's five years old.*)

Larry, Lucy. Lucy, Larry.

(*He picks up EMILY and puts her over his shoulder.*)

Have fun, kids.

(*He carries her off, EMILY shrieking in false protest.*)

LUCY: Shut the door. It's cold.

(*LARRY shuts the door gingerly.*)

I'm Lucy.

LARRY: I'm Larry.

LUCY: Nice to meet you, Larry.

(*She kisses him on the cheek.*)

LARRY: What are you doing?

LUCY: It's how people greet each other.

LARRY: In Europe maybe.

LUCY: In New York, too.

LARRY: Well I don't live either place.

This is New Jersey.

LUCY: Fine. I'm sorry. I didn't mean to make you feel
uncomfortable.

LARRY: You didn't make me feel uncomfortable.

It was unfamiliar, that's all.

There's a difference.

(*LARRY kisses her on the cheek.*)

LUCY: Hey!

(*LARRY walks around the room.*)

LARRY: This place is pretty nice.

LUCY: It's okay.

LARRY: So you live here with your parents and everything?

LUCY: It's just me and my mom. My dad, he divorced my
mom when I was two, or something.

LARRY: My parents are divorced, too.

LUCY: Really?

LARRY: But my dad remarried. So I have a stepmom. And she
had George from before so now I have a stepmom and a
stepbrother. Do you have any brothers or sisters?

LUCY: No. It's just me.

LARRY: It's better that way. More time to yourself.

LUCY: You don't like George?

LARRY: George is an asshole.

LUCY: But there's somebody around. Somebody you can play
with.

LARRY: We don't play.

He beats me up all the time. It sucks.

LUCY: That's too bad.

LARRY: It's better to be by yourself.

Trust me.

LUCY: You're probably right. But I get lonely sometimes.

LARRY: I don't get lonely.

LUCY: You don't?

LARRY: No.

I hate being around people.

I wish I could be by myself all the time.

LUCY: I'm alone all the time.

LARRY: We should trade lives.

Like in that movie.

LUCY: Yeah.

LARRY: What makes you lonely?

LUCY: I don't know.

Lots of things.

LARRY: Like what?

LUCY: Like I don't know.

Like when I'm alone.

LARRY: You can be alone and not lonely.

LUCY: I can't.

LARRY: You should learn. You'd be a lot happier.

LUCY: Thanks for the tip.

LARRY: Where do you go to school?

LUCY: I haven't started school yet.

LARRY: I just got through with pre-school.

LUCY: How was it?

LARRY: It was okay.

LUCY: I can't wait to start school.

LARRY: Yeah, it's pretty cool.

LUCY: Cool.

LARRY: I have to do it over.

LUCY: Why?

LARRY: They say I didn't have enough friends.

LUCY: You'll probably make more friends next year.

LARRY: I lied to you just then.

LUCY: Pre-school's not cool?

LARRY: No, it is. When I said I didn't have any friends– that part was true – but that's not why they're making me repeat pre-school.

LUCY: What's the real reason?

LARRY: Petty larceny.

LUCY: What's petty larceny?

LARRY: Small-time thieving.

That's what the cops call it. Petty larceny.

LUCY: What'd you steal?

LARRY: A bank shaped like a bunny. It had a slit on its head between the ears where we put money in so at the end of the year we could have a pizza party.

But I stole the bunny bank and spent all the money.

LUCY: What happened to the pizza party?

LARRY: It was cancelled.

LUCY: What'd you spend the money on?

LARRY: Chocolate.

LUCY: I love chocolate

LARRY: I ate so much I puked.

LUCY: I did that once, too.

LARRY: Anyway, that's the real reason I have to repeat pre-school and I just wanted to tell you the truth.

(*He takes off his jacket. We see bandages on his wrists.*)

LUCY: What are those?

LARRY: Bandages.

LUCY: What are they for?

LARRY: Cuts.

LUCY: How'd you get cuts on your wrists?

LARRY: That was the other reason I have to repeat pre-school.

I tried to commit suicide.

LUCY: Oh.

I've never known anyone who tried to commit suicide.

LARRY: Well now you do.

LUCY: Cool.

LARRY: At the hospital they said I was the youngest suicide attempt in the history of New Jersey.

The nurses took my picture and hung it in the lobby.

LUCY: Why'd you try to commit suicide?

LARRY: Everybody says 'enjoy your childhood while it lasts', and I'm like, 'I don't enjoy this at all.'

I'm not supposed to have a care in the world and all I can think about is how miserable life is. How much suffering there is in the world and how there doesn't seem to be any reason for it.

I figured if this is the carefree part of my life then I don't want to see the part of my life that's supposed to be hard.

So one morning before pre-school I slit my wrists with George's razor blade. But my stepmom found me.

It's too bad.

LUCY: Do you think you'll attempt suicide again?

LARRY: I don't know. I might.

If I do you can come to my funeral.

LUCY: I've never been to a funeral before.

LARRY: I've got it all planned out.

It's going to be the saddest thing in the history of America. Maybe even the world.

I'm going to commit hara-kiri, like the samurai do in Japan, but I'll still have an open casket and there will be good food like Cheetos and chocolate milk and everybody's going to cry and wonder how great my life could have been.

Will you cry?

At my funeral? If everybody else is.

LUCY: I'll try.

LARRY: That's all you can do.

Try your best.

That's what my stepmom says.

LUCY: Do you want to play Doctor with me?

LARRY: I don't know. How do you play?

LUCY: It's easy. You're the Patient and I'm the Doctor. I examine you to see what's the matter.

LARRY: But I feel fine.

LUCY: I know. It's just playing.

LARRY: Okay.

LUCY: Take your shirt off.

LARRY: No!

LUCY: How am I going to examine you with your shirt on?

LARRY: I don't know.

LUCY: Take it off.

LARRY: Fine.

(*He takes it off.*)

LUCY: What seems to be the problem?

LARRY: Nothing. I feel fine.

LUCY: I'll try again, okay?

What seems to be the problem?

LARRY: My wrists are kind of sore.

LUCY: No, not what's really the matter. Pretend.

LARRY: Oh. I'm having chest pains.

LUCY: That's very serious. Let me listen to your heart.

LARRY: Okay.

(*LUCY listens to LARRY's chest.*)

LUCY: You might need a heart transplant.

LARRY: A heart transplant!

LUCY: Do you have health insurance?

LARRY: Not that I know of.

LUCY: I'm afraid there's nothing I can do.

LARRY: But I'll die.

LUCY: I'm afraid so.

LARRY: That stinks.

LUCY: Health care in this country. What are you gonna do?

LARRY: Wait a sec. I do have health insurance.

(*He whips out an imaginary card.*)

LUCY: Wonderful!

Let's get you that new heart.

(*They do a quick heart transplant.*)

How's that new heart?

LARRY: I don't have the chest pains anymore.

LUCY: You've made a complete recovery.

Could you please slip off your pants.

LARRY: What?

LUCY: I have to check something out. It's a post-surgery thing.

LARRY: You gave me a heart transplant, Lucy, I don't see
what my pants have to do with it.

LUCY: Call me Doctor, please.

This is how you play, Larry.

I'm the Doctor and you're the Patient.

Take your pants off.

LARRY: Okay, okay.

(*He takes down his pants. He's wearing little boy underwear,
preferably red.*)

LUCY: Cough.

(*LARRY coughs. She puts her hand down his pants.*)

Cough.

(*LARRY coughs.*)

LARRY: Are you sure this is how you play Doctor?

LUCY: I'm sure.

LARRY: When I was in the hospital it wasn't like this.

LUCY: This is a private practice.

(*She takes her hand out of his pants.*)

I am finished with my examination.

You seem to be in very good shape.

I hope the heart transplant helps you live a long life.

LARRY: Thank you, Doctor.

LUCY: Now we switch.

Now you're the Doctor and I'm the Patient.

(*She lies down.*)

LARRY: Okay.

LUCY: Doctor, I'm in pain.

LARRY: Where does it hurt?

LUCY: Everywhere.

You're going to have to examine me head to toe.

(*LARRY begins to examine her.*)

3

CONCERNING COUNTLESS MORE HARDSHIPS WHICH LUCY
ENDURED WITH REGARD TO HER IMAGINARY FRIENDS, IF YOU
CAN EVEN CALL THEM THAT

LUCY and LARRY are on the couch, lying down, wrapped up in a blanket.
LUCY watches LARRY sleep. She brushes his hair with her hand.
BRADLEY appears. He's on crutches. His arm is in a sling. He has two
black eyes. His nose is bleeding. He's in really bad shape.

LUCY: Bradley!

BRADLEY: Oh, Lucy.

LUCY: It's not what it looks like.

BRADLEY: How could you?

LUCY: It just happened.

We were playing Doctor –

BRADLEY: – you played Doctor with him?

LUCY: I was lonely.

And he's the sweetest boy.

He tried to commit suicide because he said life was
meaningless.

BRADLEY: Mr Marmalade is not going to be pleased.

LUCY: He doesn't have to know.

BRADLEY: He has a right to know.

Do you know why he sent me here?

LUCY: No.

(*BRADLEY opens his briefcase.*

Takes out a box of chocolates shaped like a heart.)

BRADLEY: He wanted me to bring you these.

LUCY: Chocolates!

BRADLEY: Read the card.

LUCY: I can't read yet.

BRADLEY: I'll read it.

   (*Reading.*) Dearest Lucy,

   My heart breaks every second I'm away from you.

   All my love,

   Mr M.

   (*Not reading.*) And this is how you repay him!

   (*BRADLEY rips up the note.*)

LUCY: You don't have to tell Mr M, Bradley.

   I didn't tell anyone that he hit you.

BRADLEY: That was an accident.

LUCY: So was this. Please, Bradley. Pleeeeeeeaaase.

BRADLEY: Fine.

   I won't tell him.

LUCY: Thank you, Bradley.

BRADLEY: But don't let it happen again.

LUCY: It won't.

BRADLEY: Because Mr Marmalade cares so much about you.

   And my favorite part of this job is coming to see you.

   I would hate for that to change.

LUCY: I know. You're right. I don't know what I was thinking.

BRADLEY: Good.

   I feel better.

   We all make mistakes.

   Everyone deserves a second chance.

LUCY: Thank you, Bradley.

BRADLEY: Mr Marmalade was also wondering if he could
   change brunch on Sunday to two o'clock.

LUCY: Two o'clock is fine.

BRADLEY: Good.

   I'll pencil you in.

   (*He pencils her in.*)

   Well, I'd better be off.

   (*He begins to wobble off.*)

LUCY: What happened to you, Bradley?

BRADLEY: Skiing accident.

LUCY: You don't look so good.

BRADLEY: You should see the tree I hit.

LUCY: Are you sure everything's okay?

BRADLEY: Of course.

LUCY: You would tell me if it wasn't, right?

BRADLEY: Of course I would, Lucy.

LUCY: Take care of yourself, Bradley.

BRADLEY: You too, Lucy.

(He disappears.
She waits for LARRY to wake up.
He doesn't.
She coughs.
Nothing.
She drops something on the floor with a loud bang.
LARRY wakes up suddenly.)

LARRY: Hello.

LUCY: Hello.

LARRY: Did you sleep?

LUCY: No.

LARRY: I slept like a baby.

LUCY: You have to go.

LARRY: What?

LUCY: You have to leave now.

LARRY: Why?

LUCY: Because I said so.

LARRY: That's not a reason.

LUCY: Yes it is.

LARRY: Did I do something wrong?

LUCY: No. I can't explain. I'm sorry. You just have to leave.

LARRY: Right now?

LUCY: Right now.

LARRY: Okay.

(He gets up. Puts on his clothes.)

Can I see you again?

LUCY: No.

LARRY: Do you have a boyfriend or something?

LUCY: Sort of.

LARRY: Oh.

LUCY: What?

LARRY: I just wanted to be your boyfriend, that's all.

LUCY: Well, you can't be my boyfriend.

LARRY: Okay. No. I understand. It's just –

LUCY: What?

LARRY: Nothing.

LUCY: What is it?

LARRY: It's just...

I don't know. I've never been as happy as I am right now.

LUCY: Really?

LARRY: Yeah.

I'm sorry, I'll go.

LUCY: No. You can stay another minute.

What were you saying?

LARRY: I mean, I don't know if I've ever even been happy
before right now.

You know how earlier I was saying I don't ever get lonely?

I was lying.

LUCY: You lie a lot.

LARRY: I'm lonely all the time.

Like always.

Like for my whole life.

That's why I tried to kill myself.

But now, I'm not lonely.

I'm happy.

LUCY: I'm happy with you too, Larry.

LARRY: Then what's the problem?

(*BRADLEY appears on his crutches.*
It's important he's not in LARRY's line of vision, because LARRY
could see him...)

LUCY: It's complicated.

LARRY: No, it's simple.

LUCY: Larry, you don't understand what you're talking about. You have to go right now, okay?

LARRY: You don't want me to be your boyfriend?

LUCY: No, I'm sorry.

LARRY: I understand.

No, I don't understand.

But I'll go anyway.

LUCY: I shouldn't have played Doctor with you.

I shouldn't have led you on.

LARRY: Yeah. Okay.

Maybe I'll see you at school.

LUCY: Yeah. See you at school.

(*He's gone.*)

Are you happy?

BRADLEY: Don't be angry with me, Lucy.

I'm just doing my job.

LUCY: I'm not talking to you right now, Bradley.

BRADLEY: Let's talk about it over a cup of tea.

Do you have any tea?

LUCY: I'm fresh out.

BRADLEY: Maybe I have some.

(*He begins to open his briefcase but LUCY slams it shut.*)

LUCY: You should leave, Bradley.

BRADLEY: We have to get our stories straight, Lucy.

Mr Marmalade is going to wonder where I've been and if our stories don't match up I promise you I'll be in as much trouble as you are.

Probably more.

LUCY: Tell him the truth.

BRADLEY: Don't be ridiculous.

I'll tell him you weren't feeling well and that I made you some chicken soup.

(*GEORGE comes down the stairs, triumphant.*

EMILY follows him.)

GEORGE: Come here, I need a babysistter.

(He pinches her. She giggles.)

BRADLEY: Okay, Lucy?

Please.

EMILY: Not in front of Lucy.

GEORGE: Hiya, Lucy.

LUCY: Hello.

BRADLEY: You weren't feeling well.

I made you chicken soup.

LUCY: *(To BRADLEY.)* Fine.

GEORGE: Did you and Larry get along?

LUCY: Yes.

He's a very sweet boy.

GEORGE: Where is the little shitbird?

LUCY: He left.

GEORGE: What do you mean he left?

LUCY: I asked him to leave and he left.

Unlike some people.

BRADLEY: Mum's the word.

Goodbye, Lucy.

(BRADLEY disappears.)

GEORGE: You're fucking kidding me.

LUCY: No.

GEORGE: My parents are gonna fucking kill me.

He's suicidal you know.

LUCY: He was suicidal.

He's not anymore.

EMILY: I'm sure he's fine, George

GEORGE: Fuck do you know about it?

If there's anything wrong with him I'm gonna sue your ass,
you little bitch.

(He goes.)

EMILY: Asshole.

LUCY: How was your date upstairs?

EMILY: It was fine.

LUCY: Did you two do it?

EMILY: I'm not going to discuss it with you, Lucy.

LUCY: I hope you used protection.

EMILY: Listen, it's like ten thirty and I've got school in the
morning. I kind of have to go.

(*MR MARMALADE appears.*

He smokes a cigarette. A Newport.)

LUCY: You couldn't stay for like another half an hour?

EMILY: I'm sorry, Lucy. I can't.

Tell your mom she can pay me next time.

LUCY: Okay.

(*She goes.*)

MR MARMALADE: Good evening.

LUCY: I thought we were having brunch on Sunday.

MR MARMALADE: Some time freed up tonight.

Thought I'd drop by if that's okay.

LUCY: It's fine with me.

MR MARMALADE: You're not happy to see me?

LUCY: No, I am.

It's a surprise, that's all.

MR MARMALADE: You mind if I sit?

LUCY: Be my guest.

MR MARMALADE: Thanks.

(*He falls into the couch with a thud.*)

My feet are killing me.

(*Takes off his shoes.*)

LUCY: How was work?

MR MARMALADE: Fucking nightmare.

You have no idea.

LUCY: Have you been drinking?

MR MARMALADE: I had a few after work to unwind.

You would too if you'd ever worked a day in your life.

LUCY: I wouldn't know.

MR MARMALADE: No, you wouldn't.

LUCY: Have you made the reservations?

MR MARMALADE: Reservations for what?

LUCY: Mexico.

Cabo San Lucas.

First class across the board.

MR MARMALADE: No, I haven't made the reservations yet.

LUCY: Are you going to have Bradley do it?

MR MARMALADE: Get off my ass, all right?

Jesus.

I just got here.

I just fucking sat down and you just start nagging me about Mexico.

LUCY: We're still going to go, right?

MR MARMALADE: Sure we are.

I'll do it tomorrow, okay?

(*MR MARMALADE opens his briefcase. Takes out a vial of cocaine. He cuts two big lines. Rolls up a twenty-dollar bill.*)

LUCY: Mr Marmalade, is that cocaine?

MR MARMALADE: What? I'm sorry. You want some?

LUCY: No. I don't want any cocaine.

MR MARMALADE: Suit yourself.

(*He blows a line.*)

You sure? This is some good shit.

LUCY: I'm sure.

(*He blows the second line.*)

MR MARMALADE: Hey, let's play House.

'Hey honey, I'm home!'

LUCY: No.

MR MARMALADE: That's when you say, 'How was work?'

LUCY: I don't want to play house with you.

MR MARMALADE: And I say, 'It sucked balls. But somebody's gotta fucking provide for this fucking family you lazy bitch.'

(*Silence.*)

You don't want to play House with me?

LUCY: Not like this.

MR MARMALADE: What do you mean not like this?

LUCY: When you're drunk and high.

MR MARMALADE: What? Who's high? This is like a cup of coffee. I don't even feel it. Hey, Lucy, I work twenty hours a day you know? I gotta stay alert.

LUCY: I'm still not playing.

MR MARMALADE: Fuck that. I want to play House.

LUCY: I won't play House with you.

MR MARMALADE: Then let's play Doctor.

Come here.

My prostate hurts. I might need surgery.

LUCY: I'm not going to play Doctor with you.

MR MARMALADE: My prostate hurts.

LUCY: Get out!

MR MARMALADE: Fine.

I don't need this shit anyway.

(*He struggles to stand up.*

He opens his briefcase the wrong way. Everything falls out. Filthy porno magazines, dildos, whips, drugs, maybe an inflatable blow-up doll with the mouth open for blowjobs.)

Oh shit.

(*He gets on his hands and knees and begins to pick up the magazines and dildos.*)

These aren't even mine.

I was just holding onto them for a friend.

LUCY: Get out.

MR MARMALADE: Okay, okay. Jesus Christ.

So sorry to disturb.

I'll see you at brunch on Sunday.

LUCY: No you won't.

MR MARMALADE: What?

LUCY: I don't want to see you anymore.

MR MARMALADE: Fuck you talking about?

LUCY: I don't want to play House with you anymore.

Or Doctor.

I don't want to go to Mexico with you.

I don't want to play with you at all.

MR MARMALADE: These pornos aren't even mine, I swear.

LUCY: I don't care about the pornos.

MR MARMALADE: Because of a little coke?

LUCY: Because you're a bad person.

Because you neglect me.

Because you beat up Bradley.

Because I deserve a lot better than you.

MR MARMALADE: Is there somebody else?

LUCY: What do you mean?

MR MARMALADE: I mean is there a replacement of me?

Somebody who plays House and Doctor with you.

LUCY: No.

MR MARMALADE: You're fucking lying to me. There's
somebody else.

LUCY: There might be somebody else.

MR MARMALADE: What's his name?

LUCY: He's nobody you know.

MR MARMALADE: What's his fucking name?

LUCY: Larry.

MR MARMALADE: What the fuck kind of name is Larry?

LUCY: I don't know. It's his name.

MR MARMALADE: Fuck! I can't believe this shit.

What's this clown do?

LUCY: Do?

MR MARMALADE: Do? Do? Do? Do do do do do. What's his
fucking job? What does fucking Larry fucking do?

LUCY: He doesn't do anything.

MR MARMALADE: He's unemployed.

LUCY: He's five.

MR MARMALADE: Fuck does that mean he's five?

LUCY: He's five years old.

MR MARMALADE: Let's not go crazy here, Lucy.

You're not going to leave me for a toddler.

In business there's always a compromise.

LUCY: There's no compromise.

MR MARMALADE: I'll cut back at work.

LUCY: I'm sorry.

No.

MR MARMALADE: I'll get help for the drugs. Okay? Lucy?

I'm totally willing to admit I have a drug problem? Okay?

Twelve-step programs. Rehab. Just don't leave me.

LUCY: I'm sorry, Mr Marmalade.

MR MARMALADE: You fucking cunt.

LUCY: You're high. You don't mean what you're saying.

MR MARMALADE: Newsflash! I've been high since the

beginning, okay?

LUCY: I never meant to hurt you.

(*He hits her in the face. She falls to the ground. Her lip bleeds.*)

MR MARMALADE: You never meant to hurt me?

(*He spits on her.*

LARRY appears.)

Who the fuck is this?

(*She won't tell.*)

Answer me, bitch.

Who the fuck is this?

LARRY: I'm Larry.

LUCY: Larry?

LARRY: I'll handle this, Lucy.

MR MARMALADE: You're Larry. This is fucking Larry.

LARRY: Shut up, dude.

MR MARMALADE: Fuck you, Larry.

This is private.

LARRY: You're leaving.

MR MARMALADE: I'm not leaving.

LARRY: Yes you are.

MR MARMALADE: Who's gonna make me?

LARRY: I am.

MR MARMALADE: You and what army?

LARRY: Just me.

MR MARMALADE: Fuck you, Larry.

（*MR MARMALADE takes a swing at LARRY, but LARRY dodges it and quickly puts MR MARMALADE into a very painful submission hold.*）

LARRY: I'm a green belt in Brazilian ju-jitsu.

MR MARMALADE: Easy, Larry.

LARRY: I can break your arm in five places.

MR MARMALADE: Let's not do anything we're gonna regret, Larry.

LARRY: You think I'd regret kicking your ass?

MR MARMALADE: There will be legal ramifications. That's all I'm saying, okay?

LARRY: You're leaving.

MR MARMALADE: Owwwww. Fine. I'm leaving.

LARRY: And you're not allowed to come back. Do we understand each other, dude?

MR MARMALADE: Loud and clear, Larry. Just let go of my arm.

LARRY: You're not going to bother Lucy anymore. Right?

MR MARMALADE: Owwww. Right. Right.

（*LARRY lets go. MR MARMALADE gathers all of his magazines and dildos and puts them in his briefcase.*）

You better hope there's no nerve damage you little shit.

Expect to hear from my attorney in due course.

（*He disappears.*）

LARRY: Are you okay?

Are you bleeding?

LUCY: Maybe a little bit.

LARRY: Here, let me.

（*He dabs at the blood with a bandage from his wrist.*）

Who was that guy?

LUCY: He used to be my friend.

His name's Mr Marmalade.

LARRY: That guy was your friend?

LUCY: People change.

He used to be a good guy.

LARRY: Well he's not anymore.

LUCY: Larry?

LARRY: Yes, Lucy?

LUCY: Do you know how to play house?

INTERMISSION

4

OF WHAT HAPPENED BETWEEN LUCY AND LARRY: ONE OF THE
MOST IMPORTANT SCENES IN THIS WHOLE PLAY
P.S. IT'S LATER THAT SAME NIGHT EVEN THOUGH IT SEEMS
IMPOSSIBLE THAT YOUNG PEOPLE WOULD BE UP AT SUCH
HOURS

*LARRY enters. He's wearing his dad's suit. It's much too big for him.
He carries a child's record player with a handle.*

LARRY: Honey, I'm home!

LUCY: (*Off.*) I'm in the kitchen, honey! Just a second.

(*He turns on the record player. Greasy French romance music
plays. I suggest Yves Montand.*

*He opens his suit and takes out a big bag of potato chips,
preferably Cool Ranch Doritos.*

*He reaches into his sleeve and takes out one of those really long
liquorice ropes. Then another. Maybe another.*

*In his pants are Gummy Bears, Popsicles, candy bars, sticks
of gum, Twinkies, Ho-hos, pork rinds, Funions, Oreos, Nutter
Butters, some EZ Cheese and Redi Whip whipped cream.*

It is a cornucopia of junk food. He is very proud of his dinner.

*Wait. The last touch is a single rose which he had somewhere in
his pants. He cradles it tenderly and puts it in a vase.*

LUCY *enters. She wears the dress her mother didn't pick and most of her make-up. LUCY walks in high heels which she doesn't know how to do.)*

LARRY: Close your eyes, close your eyes.

(LUCY closes her eyes.

LARRY guides her to the table.)

Okay, open 'em.

LUCY: Oh my God!

LARRY: Dinner is served.

LUCY: Larry! It's beautiful.

LARRY: Let's just say 7-11 was kind to us.

LUCY: It looks wonderful. Thank you so much. What should we eat first?

LARRY: First, a toast.

(He pulls out some chocolate milk.)

LUCY: Chocolate milk!

LARRY: Our favorite!

(He presents it to her like it was champagne, over his arm. He lets her smell the cap. She nods in approval. LARRY pours two full glasses.)

LUCY: What are we toasting to?

LARRY: To happiness.

LUCY: To happiness.

(They clink glasses and drink.)

Mmmmm. Good, huh?

LARRY: Delicious.

LUCY: Let's eat. I'm famished.

(LARRY sits but LUCY waits by her chair.)

LARRY: Why don't you sit down?

(LUCY just stares at her chair.)

Sorry, dear.

(LARRY runs over to her chair and pulls it out for her.)

LUCY: Thank you, dear.

LARRY: My pleasure, dear.

(*LARRY unfolds her paper towel napkin and puts it in LUCY's lap.*)

Bon appetite!

(*LARRY returns to his seat and they both busily unwrap different snacks and treats. They eat for a bit.*)

LUCY: Could you pass the Doritos?

LARRY: Of course.

(*He passes the Doritos.*)

LUCY: Thank you, dear.

LARRY: My pleasure, dear.

(*LARRY pours some EZ Cheese into his mouth.*
Not be outdone, LUCY pours some whipped cream into her mouth.)

LUCY: I have some very big news, dear.

LARRY: I'm all ears.

LUCY: Are you ready?

LARRY: I think so.

LUCY: I'm pregnant.

LARRY: Really?

LUCY: I got the test results from the Doctor this afternoon.

LARRY: Are you serious?

LUCY: You're not happy!

LARRY: No, Lucy, are you for real pregnant are you play Pregnant?

LUCY: Play Pregnant.

LARRY: Oh! Wonderful news! I'm so happy! I'm going to be a father. It's mine, isn't it?

LUCY: Of course it's yours.

LARRY: That's good.

LUCY: You don't sound like you're really happy.

LARRY: Of course I'm happy.

LUCY: I know it's a bit of a shock.

LARRY: It did come as a surprise.

LUCY: But a wonderful surprise I hope.

What are you thinking about?

LARRY: I don't know if a baby is what we need right now, you know?

I don't know if I'm ready to be a father.

You know, and I don't know if I really want to bring a child into this world in general, let alone now with you. I'm not very happy that I was born and don't really feel like I'm in the position to make anyone else go through this.

LUCY: You're entitled to your opinion.

But I'm going to have it one way or another.

LARRY: Fine, you know. That's your choice.

I totally respect your right to choose.

LUCY: Good.

LARRY: Good.

Could you pass the Oreos?

LUCY: Here.

(*Gives LARRY the Oreos.*)

LARRY: Lucy?

LUCY: Yes, what is it?

LARRY: Will you feel my head?

I think I might have a fever.

(*She feels his head.*)

LUCY: You're fine.

LARRY: I think it might be my uterus.

LUCY: You don't have a uterus.

LARRY: Fine, I don't have a uterus.

It's just that we don't play Doctor anymore.

LUCY: Now we're playing House.

LARRY: So when you play House you can't play Doctor?

LUCY: That's right. They are two very different games.

LARRY: That's stupid.

LUCY: Larry!

LARRY: What? That's ridiculous.

LUCY: Can we just enjoy our dinner that you worked so hard to provide?

LARRY: I stole all this food, Lucy.

LUCY: I don't know what you're talking about.

LARRY: You know I did.

LUCY: I really don't.

LARRY: I'm not playing House anymore.

(*LARRY turns off the music.*)

LUCY: We were having such a wonderful time.

We're pregnant with our first child.

What's the matter?

LARRY: Nothing.

(*He eats.*)

LUCY: I wish you'd say something.

Tell me about work.

LARRY: It was fine.

LUCY: It wasn't too busy?

LARRY: It was fine.

(*A CACTUS and a SUNFLOWER appear.*

They can talk.)

CACTUS: Hello.

SUNFLOWER: Can we come in?

CACTUS: It's cold.

LARRY: Sure.

Come on in.

Are you hungry?

CACTUS: I'm famished.

SUNFLOWER: Me too.

LUCY: Larry?

What are those?

LARRY: Those are *my* friends.

LUCY: I thought it was going to be just you and me.

We're playing House.

LARRY: They can play House, too.

It's good to see you.

How are you guys doing?

CACTUS: I'm hungry.

SUNFLOWER: I'm cold.

CACTUS: I'm hungry and cold.

SUNFLOWER: Me too.

CACTUS: Who's the skirt?

LARRY: That's Lucy.

We're playing House.

CACTUS: She's hot.

SUNFLOWER: Good work, Larry.

LUCY: I can hear what you're saying.

CACTUS: Oh.

Excuse me.

SUNFLOWER: Nice to meet you, Lucy.

You have a beautiful home.

CACTUS: It looks like a great spread.

LUCY: I suppose there's enough food.

Even for uninvited guests.

LARRY: I didn't know they were coming.

LUCY: Can I offer you plants some chocolate milk?

CACTUS: Yes, please.

I'm very thirsty.

SUNFLOWER: I love chocolate milk.

(*She pours them glasses of chocolate milk.*)

LUCY: What should we toast to?

CACTUS: To the happy couple.

SUNFLOWER: To the happy couple.

(*They all drink.*)

LUCY: And what exactly do you plants do?

(*The PLANTS eat very messily.*)

SUNFLOWER: I just sit by the window and look at the sun.

CACTUS: Me too.

SUNFLOWER: Sometimes I think about water.

CACTUS: I think about water all the time.

LARRY: We're playing House.

CACTUS: I've never played House.

LARRY: It's easy.

SUNFLOWER: We usually play Cowboys and Indians.

I'm always the Indian.

LARRY: Just make something up.

CACTUS: Like what?

LARRY: Like a job.

CACTUS: Oh. Okay.

I'm a stuntman.

SUNFLOWER: I make submarines.

LUCY: That's very interesting.

Larry is a Banker.

He makes a very good salary and great benefits.

LARRY: Lucy!

LUCY: What? It's true, isn't it?

We're among friends. They can know how successful you are, can't they?

LARRY: I guess so.

LUCY: What have you plants been reading?

CACTUS: I don't know how to read.

SUNFLOWER: I can read my name.

LUCY: Larry just finished 'The Sound and The Fury'.

It's a very difficult book by William Faulkner.

(*The SUNFLOWER throws a piece of food.*)

Do you know who William Faulkner is?

CACTUS: Don't throw that at me, dick.

SUNFLOWER: You're the dick.

CACTUS: You're dickless.

(*They throw food at each other.*)

LUCY: Larry, stop them.

LARRY: Hey guys, take it easy.

CACTUS / SUNFLOWER: Dick!

(*They throw food at LARRY.*

LARRY throws food back.)

LARRY: You're the dicks!

(*It quickly turns into a fully fledged food fight. It's really messy.*

The vase with the flower gets knocked to the ground and breaks.
Everybody stops.)

LUCY: Get out.

CACTUS: I'm sorry.

SUNFLOWER: It was his fault.

LUCY: Get the fuck out of my house.

(*The PLANTS start crying.*)

CACTUS: We're really sorry.

SUNFLOWER: We'll be good.

CACTUS: Can we stay?

LUCY: No. I want you out of this house.

LARRY: Sorry, guys.

You heard the old ball and chain.

LUCY: You too, Larry.

LARRY: What?

LUCY: Get out.

LARRY: But…

LUCY: I don't want to play House with you anymore.

LARRY: But…

LUCY: No buts.

LARRY: Our marriage.

LUCY: It's annulled.

LARRY: What about the baby?

Shouldn't we stay together for the sake of the baby?

LUCY: It's not even yours.

SUNFLOWER: Cuckolded.

CACTUS: That's some cold shit.

LARRY: I'll see you plants later.

SUNFLOWER: Goodnight.

CACTUS: Don't let the bedbugs bite.

SUNFLOWER: I hate bedbugs.

CACTUS: Me too.

SUNFLOWER: Me three.

CACTUS: Me four.

SUNFLOWER: What's after four?

CACTUS: I don't know.

SUNFLOWER: Me neither.

(They're gone.)

LARRY: Okay, they're gone. We can keep playing.

LUCY: No, Larry.

LARRY: I'm sorry, all right?

Those plants are dicks.

I shouldn't have invited them over to play House with us.

LUCY: You should go, too.

LARRY: We can play something else.

We can play Cowboys and Indians.

LUCY: No.

LARRY: Cops and Robbers.

LUCY: No.

LARRY: Fine.

We don't have to play anything at all.

We can just sit here.

We don't even have to talk.

LUCY: I don't want you here anymore, Larry.

LARRY: We were happy!

We weren't lonely anymore.

LUCY: I was here with you, Larry, but I was still lonely.

LARRY: Oh.

Okay. I'll go.

Goodbye, Lucy.

LUCY: Goodbye, Larry.

(He goes, with his tail between his legs.

LUCY looks at the disgusting room.

Sighs and begins to clean up a little.

MR MARMALADE appears with a trash bag and rubber gloves.

He's dressed immaculately in his suit.)

MR MARMALADE: Good evening.

LUCY: What are you doing here?

MR MARMALADE: Looks like you could use an extra pair of hands.

LUCY: That would be nice.

MR MARMALADE: Allow me.

> (*He picks up the rose from the floor and gives it to her while on one knee.*)

A rose for M'lady.

LUCY: Thank you, Fair Sir.

> (*She curtsies.*
> *He cleans up all the junk food.*)

You don't have to clean up, Mr Marmalade.

MR MARMALADE: It's my pleasure.

Who made this mess?

LUCY: Larry and his plant friends.

MR MARMALADE: How is Larry?

LUCY: We broke up.

MR MARMALADE: I'm sorry to hear that.

LUCY: Yeah, right.

MR MARMALADE: No, really.

It took some getting used to, but I think you were good together.

Probably better than you and I were.

He seemed like a good guy.

LUCY: He wasn't.

> (*MR MARMALADE takes goggles out of his briefcase. Hands them to LUCY.*)

MR MARMALADE: Put these goggles on.

LUCY: I love goggles.

> (*He puts his own goggles on. She puts goggles on.*
> *MR MARMALADE whips out a large leaf-blower.*)

What's that, Mr Marmalade?

MR MARMALADE: It's my SuckBlow 6000.

LUCY: It's really big.

> (*He turns it on and blows all of the junk food off the stage. It's really loud and you shouldn't really be able to hear what he's talking about.*)

MR MARMALADE: I won it in a poker game.

LUCY: What?

MR MARMALADE: I bluffed.

> I only had a pair of twos but I just kept raising and raising until finally my friend Ramon put up this SuckBlow.
> Ramon was never much of a card player. But I think he was sort of happy to get rid of it because his ex-girlfriend Rita gave it to him so every time he blew leaves he thought of her.
>
> (*He's finished. He turns it off.*)

LUCY: What?

MR MARMALADE: Don't worry about it.

> (*He puts the SuckBlow away.*)
>
> Where were we?

LUCY: We were talking about Larry.

MR MARMALADE: I could talk to him if you want.

LUCY: Let's talk about you. How's work?

MR MARMALADE: I quit.

LUCY: You quit?

MR MARMALADE: I realized I'm not getting any younger.

> What am I doing busting my hump twenty hours a day?
> Carpe diem, you know?

LUCY: You look great.

MR MARMALADE: I went through rehab.

LUCY: Really?

MR MARMALADE: I did detox in Newark.

> Then I was in a halfway house up in New Haven for a while.

LUCY: That's wonderful, Mr Marmalade.

> I'm proud of you.

MR MARMALADE: My sponsor was an ex-junkie.

> He was blind.
> When he was using he ran out of veins so he shot up in his eyes.
> He changed my life.
> I'm sorry, you don't want to hear about all this stuff.

LUCY: No, it's fascinating.

I can't believe you've changed so much.

MR MARMALADE: I did it for you, Lucy.

LUCY: Really?

MR MARMALADE: Of course. It's always been for you.

I made you a pair of moccasins.

LUCY: No you didn't.

(*He whips out a pair of handmade moccasins.*)

MR MARMALADE: What are you, a size three?

LUCY: Three and a half.

MR MARMALADE: You've grown.

See if they fit.

(*He puts the moccasins on her feet.*)

We did all sorts of craft work at the halfway house. Basket weaving. Pottery painting. Needlepoint.

I even learned bird calling.

I can call a blue jay from fifty yards away.

(*He does a little bird call.*)

LUCY: It sounds wonderful.

MR MARMALADE: Take a walk around.

LUCY: They're nice.

Comfortable.

(*She walks.*)

MR MARMALADE: I'm sorry.

LUCY: No, they fit fine.

MR MARMALADE: No. For before. I fucked up. Excuse me. I screwed up. I was out of control.

That's step nine. Apologize to everyone I hurt when I was using.

LUCY: It seems like you've really turned over a new leaf.

MR MARMALADE: Are you willing to give me a second chance?

LUCY: Yes.

MR MARMALADE: Thank you, Lucy.

(*He picks her up and hugs her.*)

Are you hungry?

LUCY: Starving. Those plants ruined my dinner.

MR MARMALADE: Bradley!

(He snaps his fingers and BRADLEY appears with a big boat of sushi.

He looks great. No injuries at all.)

BRADLEY: Good evening, Lucy.

LUCY: Good evening, Bradley.

(LUCY looks at the sushi boat.)

MR MARMALADE: Fresh from Nobu.

Monkfish Pâté with Caviar

Sashimi Salad

Sea Urchin Tempura

Whitefish with Ponzo

Bradley's favorite, Fresh Yellowtail with Jalapeno.

BRADLEY: I love jalapeno!

LUCY: It looks delicious.

MR MARMALADE: It's all for you, Lucy.

LUCY: Thank you, Mr Marmalade.

(He snaps his fingers. Two men in white tuxedos enter with lots of roses, candelabras, champagne, fancy desserts. It's a whirlwind.)

MR MARMALADE: Roses fresh from the Garden of Versailles.

Candles handcrafted from white whale blubber.

Ice cream from the milk of cows who eat only chocolate.

LUCY: This is all for me?

MR MARMALADE: It's all for you, Lucy.

LUCY: I don't know what to say.

MR MARMALADE: Eat. Drink. Enjoy.

(She eats.)

Bradley, if you please.

(BRADLEY leads the waiters. Maybe instruments are played, if the actors know how.

A violin. A guitar. A clarinet.

They sing a sweet, slow love song all the way through.

It should be the French song from before.
BRADLEY sings in French very sweetly.
LUCY eats for a while.)

Lucy, would you do me the honor?

LUCY: It would be my pleasure.

(MR MARMALADE and LUCY dance sweetly, slowly, beautifully.
They look into each other's eyes.
She buries her head in his shoulder.
She dances on top of his shoes.
After the dance is finished, LUCY curtsies and MR MARMALADE
bows. They applaud the band.)

Thank you, Mr Marmalade.

MR MARMALADE: My pleasure.

This is the happiest night of my life.

LUCY: Mine too.

MR MARMALADE: I almost forgot. Look what I've got.

(He whips out some plane tickets.)

Mexico!

Cabo.

You and me.

We leave tonight. First class across the board!

LUCY: Mr Marmalade!

MR MARMALADE: Bradley, go get Lucy's suitcase.

(BRADLEY goes upstairs.)

That will be all for tonight, gentlemen.

Thank you very much.

(They disappear with all of the stuff they brought on.)

I missed you, Lucy.

LUCY: You did?

MR MARMALADE: Terribly.

I thought of you all the time.

It didn't matter what I was doing or who I was with.

Did you think of me?

LUCY: Yes. Always.

(He kisses her on the mouth.)

Mr Marmalade!

MR MARMALADE: Is that okay?

I'm sorry. I shouldn't have.

LUCY: No. It's okay.

MR MARMALADE: Are you sure it's okay?

LUCY: Yes. I'm sure.

MR MARMALADE: Because I've wanted to.

Before.

For a long time.

LUCY: I know.

Me too.

MR MARMALADE: Really?

LUCY: You couldn't tell?

MR MARMALADE: No. I don't know.

I thought maybe.

I didn't want to get my hopes up, you know?

LUCY: I know.

MR MARMALADE: I feel like I'm going to die when I say
goodbye to you.

LUCY: Me too.

MR MARMALADE: I don't want to leave ever again.

LUCY: I don't want you to.

MR MARMALADE: When we get back from Mexico is it all
right if I stay here with you?

LUCY: Of course.

I've always wanted you to stay.

MR MARMALADE: You have?

LUCY: I've never wanted anything else.

MR MARMALADE: This is going to be great.

LUCY: Do you want to have children?

MR MARMALADE: I want it all.

A home of our own.

A white picket fence.

Lots of kids running around.

LUCY: Me too.

That's exactly what I want.

MR MARMALADE: Everything we were promised is in our reach, Lucy.

We can be so happy.

(*BRADLEY comes back with the suitcase.*)

BRADLEY: All packed.

MR MARMALADE: Are you ready to go?

LUCY: Yes.

MR MARMALADE: Let's go.

BRADLEY: Vaminos!

(*They go.*)

5

OF WHAT HAPPENED TO LUCY AND MR MARMALADE – A SAD AND HORRIBLE SCENE IN THIS PLAY WHICH MAY BE VERY DIFFICULT TO WATCH FOR THE SQUEAMISH

A baby cries in the kitchen.

MR MARMALADE watches television. He wears a wife beater. No shoes or socks. He drinks a cheap domestic beer and smokes Newports.

The place is filthy.

Worse than before.

Beer cans. Old food. Pizza boxes.

At least a year's worth of shit and grime.

MR MARMALADE: Will you shut that kid up?

LUCY: (*Off.*) What?

MR MARMALADE: Shut the kid up!

I'm trying to watch TV.

LUCY: (*Off.*) I can't hear you, honey.

The baby's crying.

MR MARMALADE: Jesus Christ.

I know the baby's crying. I can hear the baby crying.

I want you to stop the baby from crying.

LUCY: (*Off.*) Just a second!

(*She comes dressed in her mother's slip, carrying a baby wrapped in a blanket.*)

MR MARMALADE: Leave the kid in the kitchen.

LUCY: Just tell me what you want.

MR MARMALADE: I want you to shut the fucking kid up.

LUCY: Oh.

I couldn't hear you.

MR MARMALADE: Of course you couldn't.

That kid won't stop crying.

LUCY: She won't stop crying.

I can't understand it.

(*The baby stops crying.*)

She stopped.

MR MARMALADE: Finally.

Get me a beer.

LUCY: Why don't you get one yourself?

MR MARMALADE: Fuck you.

I'm watching TV.

LUCY: It's on commercial.

MR MARMALADE: So I'm watching the commercial.

Come on, Little Mama.

Get me a beer.

LUCY: You've had enough beer.

MR MARMALADE: Don't give me that shit.

LUCY: This is your last one before dinner.

MR MARMALADE: Fine.

LUCY: Do you promise?

MR MARMALADE: I promise.

LUCY: You pinky promise?

MR MARMALADE: I pinky promise.

(*They pinky promise.*)

LUCY: If you have any more I'm gonna call your sponsor in New Haven.

(*She goes.*

He slaps her ass.)

Hey!

MR MARMALADE: Shut up, you love it.

(She leaves.

MR MARMALADE was crossing his fingers when he made the pinky promise.

LUCY comes back in with a beer.)

Open it.

(She opens it. Hands it to him.

He drinks.

She stands in the way.)

What are you doing?

I'm trying to watch TV.

LUCY: Am I standing in your way?

MR MARMALADE: You're standing right in front of the fucking TV.

LUCY: I'm sorry.

MR MARMALADE: What are you doing?

LUCY: I'm not doing anything.

MR MARMALADE: You're staring at me.

LUCY: I just like being near you, that's all.

MR MARMALADE: Go away.

I want to be by myself.

LUCY: Can't I just watch you?

MR MARMALADE: No.

Go away.

(He throws beer on her.)

LUCY: I understand.

I'll let you be.

Everybody needs time to themselves.

Call me if you need anything.

(She kisses him and leaves.

There's a moment's silence and then the baby starts crying.)

MR MARMALADE: Goddamnit!

LUCY: *(Off.)* I'm sorry, honey.

MR MARMALADE: Put a muzzle on that fucking kid!

LUCY: (*Off.*) She'll be back asleep in a minute.

MR MARMALADE: I can't take this shit anymore!

(*LUCY enters with the crying baby.*)

Shut that fucking kid up!

LUCY: She'll be asleep in a minute.

MR MARMALADE: But then she'll be awake in another minute.

LUCY: She's just teething. This will be over in a couple of months.

MR MARMALADE: Go back in the kitchen!

I can't hear myself think.

LUCY: I'm so sorry.

Just turn the television up.

(*He turns the television up.*)

MR MARMALADE: I still can't hear.

LUCY: Shhhh. Shhhh.

Be quiet.

Be quiet.

MR MARMALADE: Who's idea was it to have a kid anyway?

LUCY: She'll be quiet in a second.

Shh shhhh.

MR MARMALADE: You should have had an abortion.

LUCY: Don't say that.

MR MARMALADE: Why not?

That kid is fucking killing me.

LUCY: It was your idea to have a big family.

MR MARMALADE: Like hell it was.

LUCY: You said you wanted it all.

A house with a white picket fence.

Kids running around.

MR MARMALADE: I never said that.

LUCY: Yes you did.

MR MARMALADE: You're putting words in my mouth.

Bradley!

(*BRADLEY appears.*)

BRADLEY: What can I do for you, Mr M?

MR MARMALADE: Go upstairs and pack all my shit.

I'm leaving.

BRADLEY: Yes, sir.

(*BRADLEY goes.*)

LUCY: You can't leave!

MR MARMALADE: I can't take this shit anymore, Lucy.

LUCY: No. You can't leave.

MR MARMALADE: That kid is driving me crazy.

LUCY: She's just teething.

Things will be better in a month or two.

(*The baby stops crying.*)

You see?

MR MARMALADE: She'll be crying in like two seconds.

LUCY: I won't bother you.

I won't make a sound. I promise.

MR MARMALADE: I'm sorry.

LUCY: There must be something I can do.

MR MARMALADE: There's nothing.

LUCY: I'll clean up more.

The house will be beautiful.

(*She cleans.*)

You see?

MR MARMALADE: That's not enough.

LUCY: We can go on a vacation.

Mexico.

MR MARMALADE: I don't want to go to Mexico with a crying baby.

LUCY: We can play Doctor whenever you want.

Even in the afternoons the way you like it.

MR MARMALADE: I'm sick of playing Doctor with you.

LUCY: I won't nag you about your drinking.

Do you want another beer?

I'll go get you another beer.

MR MARMALADE: It's too late, Lucy.

LUCY: I'll be quiet. I'll be so quiet.

> You won't even know I'm alive.
>
> (*BRADLEY comes down with an enormous amount of suitcases and boxes.*
>
> *He even carries a bag in his mouth.*)

BRADLEY: (*Through a strap.*) All packed!

MR MARMALADE: Let's go.

> (*The baby starts crying.*)
>
> You see?
>
> That's what I'm fucking talking about.

LUCY: Wait! Wait!

> I can stop the baby from crying.

MR MARMALADE: Maybe for a second.

LUCY: No.

> I can stop her from crying for ever.
>
> (*She runs into the kitchen.*)

MR MARMALADE: Jesus Christ. Do you have any idea what she's talking about?

BRADLEY: (*Through a strap.*) I haven't the foggiest.

MR MARMALADE: Have you lost weight?

BRADLEY: Five pounds. I'm surprised you noticed.

MR MARMALADE: You didn't get all anorexic on me again.

BRADLEY: Of course not.

MR MARMALADE: Bradley!

BRADLEY: I'm counting calories.

> (*The baby abruptly stops crying.*
>
> *LUCY comes back in with blood all over her.*)

LUCY: You see?

> I shut her up.
>
> You can have peace and quiet.
>
> You can watch television.

MR MARMALADE: You killed her?

LUCY: Now you don't have to leave.

> You can stay here.
>
> You can rest.

I won't make a sound.

Not one little peep.

MR MARMALADE: Let's get the fuck out of here.

BRADLEY: Yes, sir!

LUCY: NO!

(BRADLEY and MR MARMALADE disappear.
She's alone.)

Don't leave me alone.

I hate being alone.

(SOOKIE and a MAN enter.
They are both pretty drunk.
They're laughing.)

SOOKIE: Shhh. Shhhh.

(They fall into something. Laughing.)

Lucy?

What are you still doing up?

MAN: You didn't tell me you have a kid.

SOOKIE: Go wait upstairs.

MAN: You didn't tell me you had a kid.

(The MAN goes.
SOOKIE sobers up.)

SOOKIE: Where's the babysitter?

LUCY: She left.

Seems like years ago.

SOOKIE: What's that on your dress?

Oh my God are you bleeding?

LUCY: It's not my blood.

SOOKIE: Whose blood is it?

LUCY: The baby's.

I killed her but he still left.

(She takes the blood and smells it.
Licks it.)

SOOKIE: That's not blood at all.

It's only ketchup.

LUCY: Fine.

It's ketchup.

SOOKIE: What are you doing pouring ketchup all over
yourself?

LUCY: It was that kind of night.

SOOKIE: Is that my slip?

LUCY: Yes.

SOOKIE: You are in big trouble young lady.

You better hope that ketchup comes out or you're gonna
get it.

LUCY: Okay.

SOOKIE: I'm serious.

I don't know what gets into you sometimes.

LUCY: Me neither.

SOOKIE: I'm going upstairs.

I am so mad at you.

LUCY: I'm sorry.

SOOKIE: You better hope that stain comes out.

LUCY: I'll hope.

SOOKIE: What?

LUCY: I said I'll hope.

SOOKIE: You better.

Or you're gonna get it.

(*She goes upstairs.*

LUCY is alone.)

6

THE FINAL SCENE IN THIS PLAY WHICH CONCERNS LUCY'S
RESOLUTION WITH MR MARMALADE, WHICH ENDS IN DEATH,
WHICH IS WHERE ALL STORIES END IF YOU FOLLOW THEM LONG
ENOUGH

Morning. LUCY plays with two Barbies. She wears her tutu and tights.
BRADLEY appears. Maybe BRADLEY is already in the room.

LUCY: Get out of here, Bradley.

BRADLEY: I know you probably don't want to see me.

LUCY: You're right.

BRADLEY: I've come with news.

LUCY: I hope Mr M didn't send you on some peace mission

because it's not going to work.

I never want to see him again.

BRADLEY: He didn't, Lucy.

LUCY: Then what are you doing here?

BRADLEY: Mr Marmalade committed suicide.

LUCY: Oh my God.

BRADLEY: I found him this morning.

LUCY: How'd he do it?

BRADLEY: Hara-kiri.

LUCY: When's the funeral?

BRADLEY: It was this morning. You weren't invited.

He was cremated and I spread his ashes over the Hudson.

And then I sang 'Stairway to Heaven'.

Everyone said it was a beautiful service.

LUCY: It sounds nice.

BRADLEY: He left you this note.

(He reaches into his briefcase and takes out a note. It looks one thousand years old.
He gives it to LUCY, who reads.

MR MARMALADE appears, not in the living room, perhaps in ceremonial kimono.)

MR MARMALADE: Dearest Lucy,

I had everything I'd ever wanted.

A house with a white picket fence.

A newborn baby.

A beautiful wife.

But it didn't make me happy.

So I threw it all away.

And now I can't live with myself.

When you think of me I hope you remember only the good things.

I hope you remember Mexico, which was the happiest time of my life.

Yours forever,

Mr Marmalade.

(MR MARMALADE commits hara-kiri.

He disappears.)

LUCY: Do you have a lighter?

BRADLEY: Zippo or childproof?

LUCY: Zippo.

(He reaches into his briefcase.

Gives her the Zippo.)

Do you have a coffee can?

BRADLEY: I do as a matter of fact.

(He reaches back into the briefcase and takes out a coffee can.

Gives it to her.

LUCY lights the suicide note and puts it in the coffee can.)

What are you doing?

LUCY: I'm burning it.

BRADLEY: Don't you want to keep it?

LUCY: No.

I want to forget I ever knew him.

(The one-night stand MAN enters. He tries to sneak out.)

Good morning.

MAN: Good morning.

Sarah, right?

LUCY: Lucy.

MAN: Right. Lucy.

Sorry.

LUCY: What's your name?

MAN: My name's Bob.

LUCY: How old are you, Bob?

MAN: I'm thirty-four.

How old are you?

LUCY: I'm four.

MAN: Four!

That must be nice.

LUCY: It's a walk in the park.

BRADLEY: The irony!

MAN: Wait till you're my age. Things are totally different.

LUCY: I probably won't live till I'm your age.

I'm probably going to commit suicide.

BRADLEY: Don't say that, Lucy!

MAN: Okay. Awkward.

Will you tell your mom I had to go?

LUCY: Tell her yourself, Bob.

MAN: Right.

I'm just gonna go.

(*He exits.*)

LUCY: Asshole.

BRADLEY: You're not going to commit suicide, are you, Lucy?

LUCY: No. I was just playing.

BRADLEY: That's a relief.

I have to be going too, Lucy.

It was wonderful to see you again.

Keep in touch.

LUCY: Wait, Bradley.

SOOKIE: (*Off.*) Lucy!

LUCY: In here!

Can you wait two seconds, Bradley.

BRADLEY: I suppose.

(*Counting.*) One, two.

Just kidding.

(*SOOKIE enters, dressed for work. Maybe she's a waitress.*)

SOOKIE: Good morning.

(*She kisses LUCY on the head.*)

LUCY: Good morning.

SOOKIE: Good morning, Mr Marmalade! Is he here?

Are you guys doing espresso?

LUCY: No, Mom. Mr Marmalade is dead.

SOOKIE: Oh.

LUCY: He killed himself.

He committed harey karey.

BRADLEY: (*Correct pronunciation.*) Hara-kiri.

LUCY: Hara-kiri.

SOOKIE: I'm sorry to hear that.

LUCY: Mr Marmalade's personal assistant is here.

BRADLEY: Former personal assistant.

LUCY: Former personal assistant.

SOOKIE: Tell him hello for me.

BRADLEY: It is a pleasure to finally make your acquaintance.

SOOKIE: What smells like it's been burning?

LUCY: I burned Mr Marmalade's suicide note.

SOOKIE: Goddamnit, Lucy.

You'd better clean it up.

And you'd better clean the ketchup off my slip before I get home.

LUCY: Bob had to leave.

SOOKIE: Oh.

Yes. Bob is a friend from work.

Which is where I have to go.

Mrs Ramirez is going to be forty-five minutes late. Can you hold down the fort until then?

LUCY: I think I can handle it.

SOOKIE: I'll see you at six tonight.

(*She goes.*)

LUCY: What are you going to do now, Bradley?

BRADLEY: I haven't the foggiest.

I feel like a ship lost at sea.

I don't even have a reference from Mr Marmalade.

The job market is horrible with this economy.

(*SOOKIE comes back in.*)

SOOKIE: Lucy, there's a boy outside. Says his name's Larry.

Do you know a boy named Larry?

LUCY: I did a long time ago.

What's he want?

SOOKIE: He was wondering if you'd like to go outside and
play.

LUCY: Did he mention what he'd be playing exactly?

SOOKIE: I think he said Dodgeball.

LUCY: Dodgeball.

I've never played it.

BRADLEY: It's a good game.

You should play.

SOOKIE: What do you want me to tell Larry?

LUCY: Tell him I'll think about it.

SOOKIE: Okay.

See you after work.

Don't forget to wear your coat. It's getting nippy.

(*She goes outside.*)

BRADLEY: I'd better get going, too.

Start the job hunt.

LUCY: Bradley, you could stay here if you want.

BRADLEY: Really?

LUCY: Sure. I can't pay you much.

BRADLEY: What kind of benefits package do you have?

LUCY: I think it's pretty good.

BRADLEY: Dental?

LUCY: Sure.

BRADLEY: 401(k)?

LUCY: Yup.

BRADLEY: I can type eighty words per minute.

I'm really good with schedules.

And I know PowerPoint if you need to make presentations.

LUCY: That's okay. You can just live here. I don't make
    presentations or anything.

BRADLEY: Are you sure?

LUCY: Yes.

BRADLEY: What will I do?

LUCY: Whatever you want.

BRADLEY: Whatever I want?

I don't know what I want.

LUCY: You'll figure it out as you go.

BRADLEY: Okay. It's a deal.

LUCY: Okay.

(*LARRY comes in carrying a yellow dodgeball.*
He has a black eye.)

LARRY: Hi, Lucy.

LUCY: Hi, Larry.

LARRY: Could you give us a minute in private?

BRADLEY: Is he talking to me?

LUCY: Yes.

BRADLEY: Of course.

I'll just be in the kitchen.

LUCY: Thanks, Bradley.

BRADLEY: You should put a cold steak on that black eye.

(*BRADLEY goes into the kitchen.*)

LARRY: Last night I tried to hang myself with my belt.

I was up on a chair, I had the belt wrapped around my
neck.

I was about to kick the chair out from under me when
George comes in and he's like, 'What the fuck are you
doing, Larry?' and he took me down and beat me up.
That's where I got this black eye.

LUCY: I'm sorry George beat you up.

LARRY: No, it was good.

I was happy.

Because I realized when he was beating me up that I didn't want to die.

And that I wanted to come by this morning to see if you wanted to play Dodgeball but I totally understand if you don't because you've got company and all.

But the thing is we can do it some other time, because –

LUCY: – I'm going to play Dodgeball with you, Larry.

LARRY: You are?

LUCY: I am.

LARRY: Cool.

Okay.

I'll just wait outside.

LUCY: Okay.

LARRY: Okay.

See you in a minute.

LUCY: See you in a minute.

(*He goes outside.*)

Bradley, you can come back.

(*BRADLEY comes back.*)

BRADLEY: He certainly was talkative, wasn't he?

LUCY: He had a lot to say.

BRADLEY: You're going to play Dodgeball with him?

LUCY: Yes.

BRADLEY: I think you're going to like it.

It's a good game.

LUCY: How do I look?

BRADLEY: You look beautiful.

LUCY: Thank you, Bradley.

(*BRADLEY helps her with her coat.*)

BRADLEY: Do you want me to stay here?

LUCY: If you would like to.

BRADLEY: I would.

LUCY: Just make yourself at home.

BRADLEY: Okay.

LUCY: So, I'll see you later.

BRADLEY: See you later.

> (*She goes.*
> *BRADLEY walks around the room.*
> *Touches the furniture.*
> *Straightens things up a bit.*
> *He takes off his shoes.*
> *Sees the La-Z-Boy.*
> *Gets on it.*
> *Pulls the lever to recline and then again to return upright. He does this a couple times, having a hoo-ha of a time.*
> *BRADLEY lies back as the lights slowly fade.*
> *Maybe BRADLEY sings during the curtain call like in 'Twelfth Night'.*)

THE END

VIGILS

for Gillian, who left

Characters

WIDOW, a widow.

SOUL, her husband's soul. The eternal part of him.

WOOER, a youngish suitor. Strapping.

BODY, the widow's husband's body. It plays scenes from their life.

CAPTAIN O'REILLY, wears a moustache.

GRANDFATHER, the widow's grandfather.

CHILD

NOTE

This play makes many quick shifts in time, which could or could not be reflected in costume. There is also quite a bit of flying. I think both costume changes and getting into / out of flying harnesses can be done onstage, with the help of people in black wearing headsets. Oh. And I say that the lights go out and come back on a lot. But I don't mean blackouts. Blackouts make me a little queasy.

DOUBLING

Captain O'Reilly is played by the actor who plays the Body. Grandfather is played by the actor who plays the Soul.

Vigils was first performed on 14 October 2006 at the Goodman Theatre, Chicago, with the following company:

WIDOW, Johanna Day
SOUL, Marc Grapey
WOOER, Coburn Goss
BODY, Steve Key

Directed by Kate Whoriskey
Set and costume design by Walt Spangler
Lighting design by Jason Lyons
Original music and sound design by Rob Milburn &
                                    Michael Bodeen
Projections Designer John Boesche
Choreographer Randy Duncan
Dramaturg Tanya Palmer
Production Stage Manager Kimberly Osgood

Scene One

A bedroom on the second floor. From the window you can see the ocean.
Maybe a seagull flies by.
There's a bed, a portrait of the WIDOW's dead husband, which is actually
the actor playing the BODY, and a box for the SOUL. There's a bathroom
that we can see a little bit of.
The WIDOW stands by the window, waiting.
She's dressed up. A new purple dress. Heels, which make a click clack on
the wood floor. She has a gin and tonic. She swirls it so the ice makes a
tinkle tinkle noise on the edge of the glass.
The SOUL sits in an overstuffed chair.
It's dressed all in black, maybe some leather, but not too S&M.
It doesn't have any eyes.

WIDOW: It's been two years since you died.

  It was fall, like it is now, and the leaves had already fallen.
  Not that much has changed. I still drink gin and tonic. I
  still believe happiness never really lasts, I still watch the
  'Macy's Thanksgiving Day Parade', and I still love you.
  I've tried my best not to. I've tried so hard to forget.

SOUL: I know you've tried.

WIDOW: Every day I wake up and think maybe today is the
  day I won't remember.

  And it never is. Every day is the same.

  I wear the same black dress. I walk around in the same
  circles. One of these days I'm going to wear a hole in the
  floor.

SOUL: Today is different.

WIDOW: Yes, today I'm wearing a brand new purple dress,
  waiting to be picked up for my first date since you died.

SOUL: Are you nervous?

WIDOW: I told myself I wasn't going to be. But I am.

  I don't think I can make small talk anymore.

SOUL: So make big talk.

WIDOW: What's big talk?

SOUL: Ask him if he thinks happiness really lasts.

Ask him if he believes in an afterlife.

Ask him if he thinks each person's soul is judged for the things they do on earth.

WIDOW: Nobody wants to talk about that stuff on a first date.

That'll totally freak him out.

SOUL: Fine.

Talk about the weather.

Talk about whatever you like.

WIDOW: Do you think you're going to be judged for what you did on earth?

(*A baby cries. Only the SOUL hears it.*)

SOUL: I don't know.

(*The BODY appears. In fireman outfit. He has an axe.*)

I hope not.

(*The BODY runs from one side of the room to the other and chops down a door.*

It climbs through.

The baby stops crying.

The WOOER appears at the door looking nervous holding flowers. He wears a suit and tie, which he is unaccustomed to.

He knocks on the door.)

WIDOW: He's here.

(*Calling.*) I'll just be a minute! I just got out of the shower!

WOOER: (*Calling.*) Take your time!

(*Outside the door the WOOER sprays breath freshener in his mouth. He checks his hair. He makes sure his underarms don't smell.*)

WIDOW: Let's practice my small talk.

So, did you catch the game last night?

SOUL: No. I don't have any eyes. I'm a soul.

WIDOW: No. That was small talk.

I'll start over.

So, did you catch the game last night?

SOUL: Yeah.

It sure was a good game.

WIDOW: That's what I thought.

But I think their defense is slipping.

SOUL: I think the best defense is a good offense.

WIDOW: I have to disagree with you.

I think a team with sound defense, while not as flashy as a team with a high-powered offense, is more rooted in the fundamentals of the game and therefore the better team.

SOUL: You make a very good case for the importance of defense.

I change my opinion.

WIDOW: That was pretty good small talk.

Let's try the weather.

You go.

SOUL: So.

Fall sure came early this year, huh?

WIDOW: Sure did.

My husband died in the fall.

So when I see the leaves fall I think of his death.

Even though it's been two years already it seems like only yesterday he was alive and he held me in his arms and we were happy.

(*She starts crying.*)

SOUL: Maybe you should avoid talking about the weather.

WIDOW: You're right.

I'll stick to sports.

SOUL: Or you could talk about the restaurant

The food.

WIDOW: That's a great idea.

What else do people talk about?

SOUL: Movies. Celebrity gossip. The weather.

WIDOW: But I'm avoiding the weather.

SOUL: Right. You're avoiding the weather.

WIDOW: And I don't go to the movies anymore.

That was something you and I did together and it makes me so sad.

Even the smell of popcorn makes me cry.

SOUL: Celebrity gossip?

WIDOW: I don't know who's a celebrity anymore.

SOUL: Then I guess you should stick to sports.

WIDOW: I'm not ready for this.

SOUL: Yes you are.

Just open the door.

WIDOW: What if I start crying?

SOUL: Say you have to powder your nose.

WIDOW: Powder my nose. Got it.

SOUL: Open the door.

WIDOW: Wish me luck.

SOUL: You don't need luck.

WIDOW: Wish me luck anyway.

SOUL: Good luck.

WIDOW: Thank you.

(*She opens the door.*)

Sorry that took so long.

WOOER: It was worth the wait.

You look beautiful.

(*The WOOER kisses the WIDOW on the cheek.*
She blushes.)

Hey.

SOUL: What's up?

WIDOW: Are those flowers for me?

WOOER: Yes, they are.

I bought them from my cousin who's a professional florist.

WIDOW: They're beautiful.

I love roses.

(*She puts the roses in water.*)

SOUL: That's not true.

You love marigolds.

WOOER: You don't love roses?

WIDOW: I love marigolds *and* roses.

SOUL: Since when?

WIDOW: I can love two kinds of flowers, can't I?

SOUL: Of course you can, that's just news to me.

WOOER: You don't have to pretend to love them.

I asked my cousin what kind of flowers to bring and he asked me, 'Do you like this girl' and I said, 'This isn't a girl, this is a woman', and he asked me, 'Do you like this woman' and I said, 'You better believe I do', and he said buy her twelve long-stemmed roses so I did.

It's not like I have a personal affinity for roses. I was just going on his say-so because he's a professional florist, but to be honest they were the most expensive flower in the flower shop and he works on commission so I think he was trying to stiff me. We were really never that close to begin with.

WIDOW: Can I fix you a drink?

WOOER: I would love one but I don't know if we have the time.

I heard (*Mispronouncing the name.*) Chez Genevieve is stingy about their reservations.

WIDOW: We have reservations at (*Correct pronunciation.*) Chez Genevieve?

WOOER: I hope that's okay.

WIDOW: It's more than okay.

It's just such an extravagance.

WOOER: I'm gonna pay for dinner and everything, if that's what you're worried about.

WIDOW: It's not.

SOUL: It's where we got engaged.

WOOER: Oh.

Then we'll go somewhere else.

WIDOW: Don't be silly.

SOUL: Those reservations are impossible to get.

And I barely even remember when I proposed.

WIDOW: You don't remember when you proposed?

SOUL: (*Sotto voce.*) Of course I do.

I was just saying that to make it less awkward.

WOOER: (*Sotto voce.*) This might be rude, but can we talk about this not right in front of your husband's soul?

It's weirding me out.

WIDOW: Of course we can.

SOUL: I should be getting in bed anyway.

(*The SOUL gets in the box, which hopefully doesn't look too much like a coffin.*)

I hope your date goes well.

WIDOW: Have a good night's sleep.

SOUL: I'm glad it's you. You were always my favorite.

WOOER: Thank you.

Sorry, I don't know what to call you, anymore.

SOUL: Soul is fine.

WOOER: Thank you, Soul.

WIDOW: Goodnight.

(*The WIDOW kisses the SOUL on the head, like you do with a child.*)

SOUL: Goodnight.

(*The SOUL ducks down.*

The WIDOW locks the lock with a key from around her neck.)

WOOER: Let's seriously just go somewhere else.

WIDOW: Those reservations are impossible to get.

WOOER: I just thought you would like something fancy.

And since I'm not exactly the fanciest guy I asked my cousin, a different cousin, a real estate broker who knows everything about nightlife: I asked him, 'What's the fanciest place in town' and he said 'Chez Genevieve', and I asked him, 'Is it hard to get reservations' and he said, 'Impossible.'

And I thought that's what you would want. Somewhere fancy that's hard to get into.

But me, I'm more of a simple kind of guy.

I would be fine just eating tacos down at Ernesto y Ernesto.

WIDOW: You mean at that little taco shop down by the river.

WOOER: That's the one.

WIDOW: I've always wanted to go there but I thought I'd get mugged.

WOOER: It looks a little rough but the food is amazing.

The guys who run it are two brothers, both named Ernesto, which is where they got the name.

WIDOW: I figured.

WOOER: They swam to America all the way from Ecuador on just a surfboard.

The older Ernesto got half his arm bit off by a shark.

But he can still make a mean taco.

WIDOW: You really don't mind if we skip Chez Genevieve?

(*The WOOER takes off his tie and puts it in his pocket.*)

WOOER: Do I mind?

I hate wearing a tie. To tell you the truth I can't even tie one.

I had to ask my cousin to tie it for me.

WIDOW: The florist or the real estate broker?

WOOER: A different one.

A kindergarten teacher who was the first girl I ever kissed.

I know that's illegal but we were only eight.

WIDOW: How many cousins do you have?

WOOER: I lost count.

I think it's in the mid to high twenties.

WIDOW: I wish I had more family.

Because that's all you have in the end.

WOOER: I don't know if that's exactly true.

WIDOW: That's what people say anyway. I wouldn't know.

My husband was my only family and he's been dead now for over two years. He died at the beginning of fall, just like it is now. But I guess you already knew that.

WOOER: I guess I did.

WIDOW: Excuse me. I have to powder my nose.

(*She goes quickly into the bathroom.*)

WOOER: Take your time.

Ernesto y Ernesto are open late.

(*The WOOER pokes around the room.*

Checks out the view from the window. The picture of the dead husband.)

(*Calling into the bathroom.*) You two never thought about having any children?

WIDOW: (*Calling back.*) What?

(*They speak loudly through the door until she comes out.*)

WOOER: You said he was your only family. I was just wondering if you two ever thought about having children.

WIDOW: I had a miscarriage a long time ago. Sometimes at night I think I can hear my baby crying.

WOOER: I'm so sorry. I had no idea you had a miscarriage.

WIDOW: It's not your fault.

How could you have known?

WOOER: I know, but I'm sorry anyway.

WIDOW: Thanks.

That's sweet of you to say.

(*The WIDOW comes back, sort of fresh but sort of streaky with make-up.*)

WOOER: You look really beautiful.

Did I already tell you that?

WIDOW: You did.

WOOER: Oh.

Sorry.

Sometimes when I get nervous I repeat myself.

WIDOW: You don't have to apologize.

WOOER: I'm not very good at small talk.

WIDOW: You're not?

WOOER: No. I can't stand it when people talk about sports or gossip or the weather.

WIDOW: Me neither.

WOOER: I just wanted to tell you that tonight means a lot to
me.

WIDOW: It means a lot to me, too.

WOOER: You don't have to say that.

WIDOW: I'm not just saying it.

SOUL: (*From inside the box.*) She's not!!

WOOER: You can hear us, Soul.

SOUL: Sorry!!

I should have pretended that I can't!!

WOOER: (*Quietly.*) Can we get out of here?

WIDOW: (*Quietly.*) Yes.

I can't wait to meet the Ernestos.

WOOER: (*Quietly.*) They're gonna love you.

Do you speak Spanish?

WIDOW: (*Quietly.*) No.

Do you?

WOOER: (*Quietly.*) Solamente hablo un poco de espanol.

WIDOW: (*Quietly.*) What's that mean?

WOOER: (*Quietly.*) I'll tell you on the way.

(*He offers his arm.*
She takes it and they go.
The lights fade.
Once they're black we hear a baby crying.
And smoke comes out from under the door.
The BODY appears in fireman outfit, carrying an axe.)

SOUL: I could hear a baby crying inside so I axed down the
door.

(*The BODY axes down the door. Goes inside.*)

Even though it couldn't possibly understand me I call out
to it.

I say, 'Hold on. I'm coming.'

(*The BODY comes out into a smoky room.*)

BODY: Hold on.

I'm coming.

SOUL: My last thoughts were, in order:

I'll find the baby.

People will call me a hero.

I'll say humbly:

BODY: I'm just doing my job.

SOUL: I think about my wife. About the way her face looks in the morning, before she's awake.

The way her lips curl down.

I think, 'Where is that baby.'

BODY: Where is that baby?

SOUL: How much smoke has it inhaled?

BODY: How much smoke has it inhaled?

SOUL: Even though it couldn't understand me I call out to it.

I say, 'Hold on. I'm coming.'

BODY: Hold on.

I'm coming.

SOUL: I think about the time my wife had a miscarriage.

I think about what I would have named my child.

Whether I would have made a good father.

I think about whether people are born good and the world makes them evil or whether some people are born evil and stay that way.

I wonder whether there is a judgement of souls for what they did on earth.

And if there is, I wonder whether I'll go to heaven or to hell.

And I think about the baby. Who stopped crying.

(*The baby stops crying.*)

BODY: Don't stop crying!

Let me hear you cry!

SOUL: My last thought is about the big red spot on Jupiter, which somebody told me once is actually a huge storm, twice as big as the earth.

BODY: That's one big storm.

SOUL: And then the roof falls on me.

(*The roof collapses.*

The lights go to black, except for on the SOUL.)

SOUL: And my body dies.

(Lights go down on the BODY.

Lights come up on the BODY masturbating to a filthy magazine.)

That's me masturbating.

It's a little embarrassing.

(The WIDOW enters.)

WIDOW: Oh my God!

BODY: Oh my God!

Don't you knock?

WIDOW: How could I have known?

Should I let you keep going.

BODY: No. I'm not really in the mood anymore.

(Lights down on the BODY and the WIDOW.

Lights up on the BODY and the WIDOW. The BODY thinks of nothing at all.)

SOUL: This is me thinking about nothing at all.

WIDOW: What are you thinking about?

BODY: What?

WIDOW: What are you thinking about?

BODY: Nothing at all.

(He thinks about nothing at all.

Lights down on the BODY and the WIDOW.

Lights come up on the BODY and the WIDOW having sex doggy-style.)

SOUL: That's me and my wife having sex.

She liked doggy-style the best, but I liked looking into her eyes.

When I couldn't look into her eyes I found myself fantasizing about somebody else.

WIDOW: What are you thinking about?

BODY: Baseball.

(The BODY comes.)

SOUL: I kind of had a problem with premature ejaculation.

I always apologized.

BODY: I'm sorry.

SOUL: She said:

WIDOW: It's fine.

> We'll try again next week.
>
> (*They go to sleep.*)

SOUL: We're sleeping.

> Look at how she stole the covers.
>
> Seriously. She was a different person when she was asleep and that person was evil.
>
> (*The WIDOW steals the covers.*)
>
> I'm dreaming I can fly. I'm high above my house.
>
> (*The BODY flies.*)
>
> I can see everybody I know.

BODY: Hello down there!

SOUL: I fly over the ocean and see the barges carrying cars and timber.

> I fly next to a transatlantic airplane and see what movie they're watching.

BODY: That's one of my favorites!

SOUL: I fly to the North Pole, where Superman had his crystal palace in 'Superman II'.

> And then I wake up.
>
> (*It's the morning. The WIDOW lies in bed reading a magazine. The BODY gets ready for work. He turns on the shower, and brushes his teeth.*)
>
> This is the morning after a fight.

BODY: I don't know what you want me to say.

WIDOW: I don't want you to say anything.

BODY: I said I was sorry.

WIDOW: I heard you.

SOUL: We were never very good at fighting.

BODY: I apologized. You're supposed to say it's okay.

WIDOW: It's okay.

BODY: You have to mean it.

WIDOW: But I don't.

BODY: Fuck this. I have to get ready for work.

(*The BODY goes into the shower.*

The WIDOW gives him the middle finger once he's in the shower.)

SOUL: That was not one of my finer moments.

I should have told her I loved her.

But instead I sang 'Killing Me Softly' in the shower.

(*The BODY sings 'Killing me Softly' in the shower.*)

I never had much of a voice but I liked the way it sounded echoed off the tile.

(*The WIDOW puts Kleenex in her ears.*

The BODY appears as a boy.

He has a BB gun.)

This is the worst thing I ever did.

I'm twelve years old.

We had this evil old neighbor, Mrs Van Haften.

(*The WIDOW, as Mrs Van Haften, cackles.*)

SOUL: We weren't allowed in her backyard so any balls that went over her fence were gone forever.

WIDOW: They're gone forever.

(*She cackles.*)

SOUL: I was just going to scare her.

BODY: Take that Mrs Van Haften

SOUL: But I got too close.

(*The BODY shoots out a window. It breaks. The WIDOW screams.*)

BODY: Oh fuck.

(*And then a siren. The BODY runs.*)

SOUL: She lost her eye.

And then a month or so later she died.

Not that the two were related. But it felt like they were.

I felt like I murdered her, and for years I would put fresh flowers on her grave.

(*The WIDOW appears aged about seventeen. She wears a poodle skirt.*

Music rises.)

This is the first night I laid eyes on my wife. At the Valentine's dance in high school.

She could barely see without her glasses.

WIDOW: I can barely see without my glasses.

(The WIDOW bumps into something.)

SOUL: There I am.

(The BODY appears in a tie.)

Was I really that handsome?

BODY: You better believe it.

(The BODY checks its hair in something reflective.)

SOUL: And then I see her from across the room.

(The WIDOW bumps into something else.)

And I walk across the room and ask her to dance.

BODY: Do you wanna dance or something?

SOUL: She says yes.

WIDOW: I guess so.

(They dance.)

SOUL: She isn't a very good dancer.

(She steps on the BODY's foot.)

BODY: Owww.

WIDOW: Sorry.

SOUL: I couldn't think of anything to say. How was I supposed to know this was the woman I'd spend the rest of my life with? All I knew is that I was happy.

I said so.

BODY: I'm happy.

SOUL: She said:

WIDOW / SOUL: Me too.

BODY: Owww.

WIDOW: Sorry.

SOUL: I ask her if she wanted to go outside.

(The BODY whispers into the WIDOW's ear, who giggles. They leave.)

We end up having sex in the back seat of her car.

A couple of months later she got pregnant and we got married.

But then she had a miscarriage.

And I thought do we still have to be married?

But I felt bad asking for a divorce.

She was depressed and I couldn't leave her.

We stuck it out and some days were good and some days were bad.

(*The WIDOW appears setting the table for dinner.*)

This is Thanksgiving dinner.

We are setting the table.

(*The BODY appears.*)

BODY: Does the fork go on the left or the right?

SOUL: I was never very helpful, domestically speaking.

(*The BODY drops something.*)

WIDOW: Why don't you just sit down?

SOUL: Time passes.

(*Time passes.*)

It's after dinner.

I tell a joke.

BODY: So then the shell says to the crab, 'Wouldn't you like to know?'

SOUL: And we both laugh.

(*They both laugh.*)

BODY: Can I get some more of that stuffing?

SOUL: This is happiness.

WIDOW: There's plenty more stuffing.

SOUL: It's not some time in the future.

WIDOW: My grandmother taught me to make the gravy without any lumps.

SOUL: This very second.

BODY: What's the secret?

SOUL: Inside every second is an eternity.

WIDOW: I'll never tell.

SOUL: And then the moment passes.

(*The lights go down.*

Lights up on the BODY masturbating to an even dirtier magazine.)

That's me masturbating again.

I'm sorry but these memories come in no particular order.

Why can't I just remember the happy times?

BODY: We're not in control of what we remember and what we forget.

(*The WIDOW enters.*)

WIDOW: Oh my God!

BODY: Oh my God!

SOUL: Oh my God!

BODY: Don't you knock?

WIDOW: I'm sorry.

Do you want to finish?

BODY: Yes. Thank you.

(*She goes.*)

SOUL: And I finish.

(*The BODY comes.*

Lights go down on the BODY.)

What's next?

I hope it's not any more masturbating.

But it could be.

I don't know what I'm going to remember next.

(*Lights up on the BODY playing the harmonica.*

Badly.)

I can't play the harmonica.

But I wish that I could. I remember trying.

BODY: I can't find the right note.

SOUL: There is no right note.

There's just one note and then another.

One moment and then the next.

And the moments accrue.

BODY: I can find it.

SOUL: I'm not going to remember this anymore.

BODY: Wait. I can find the right note.

SOUL: There is no such thing.

BODY: Let me try.

SOUL: I'm sorry.

> (*Lights down on the BODY.*
>
> *Lights up on the WIDOW and the WOOER.*)

WOOER: I was just wondering if you two ever thought about having children.

WIDOW: I had a miscarriage a long time ago. Sometimes at night I think I can hear my baby crying.

SOUL: This is earlier tonight. You remember, it was near the beginning.

WOOER: I'm so sorry. I had no idea you had a miscarriage.

WIDOW: It's not your fault.

How could you have known?

SOUL: How could he have known?

WOOER: I know, but I'm sorry anyway.

WIDOW: Thanks.

That's sweet of you to say.

WOOER: You look really beautiful.

Did I already tell you that?

WIDOW: You did.

WOOER: Oh.

Sorry.

Sometimes when I get nervous I repeat myself.

WIDOW: You don't have to apologize.

SOUL: His sincerity is not an affectation.

WOOER: I'm not very good at small talk.

WIDOW: You're not?

SOUL: He cares for my wife.

WOOER: No.

I can't stand it when people talk about sports or gossip or the weather.

WIDOW: Me neither.

SOUL: For the first time I can hear hope in my wife's voice.

WOOER: I just wanted to tell you that tonight means a lot to
me.

WIDOW: It means a lot to me, too.

SOUL: She can be happy without me.

She can forget me.

WOOER: You don't have to say that.

WIDOW: I'm not just saying it.

SOUL: And from inside the box I yelled; you remember:

She's not!!

WOOER: You can hear us, Soul.

SOUL: From inside the box I yelled:

Sorry!!

I should have pretended that I can't!!

WOOER: (*Quietly.*) Can we get a doubt of beer?

WIDOW: (*Quietly.*) Yes.

I can't plate to feet the Ernestos.

SOUL: I don't think that is what they said.

But I couldn't hear them.

They were talking so quietly and I was in the box.

WOOER: (*Quietly.*) Pear funnel love shoe.

To shoe seek Spanish?

WIDOW: (*Quietly.*) No.

To shoe?

WOOER: (*Quietly.*) Slowly Pablo made one poke desperado.

WIDOW: (*Quietly.*) What's rat queen?

WOOER: (*Quietly.*) I'll fell shoe on tree day.

(*He puts his arm out.*

She takes it and they leave.)

SOUL: And she takes his arm and they leave and eat tacos
down by the river.

The Ernestos story is amazing, and the tacos are delicious.

He's nervous and charming.

She laughs at his jokes.

She forgets about me for minutes at a time.

For minutes at a time she's happy.

Her memory of me is already fading.

(*The baby cries.*

The room fills with smoke.

The BODY axes down the door and goes in.)

Even though it couldn't understand me I call out to it.

I say, 'Hold on. I'm coming.'

(*The BODY comes out into a smoky room.*)

BODY: Hold on.

I'm coming.

SOUL: My last thoughts:

People will call me a hero.

I'll say humbly:

BODY: I'm just doing my job.

SOUL: I think about my wife. About the way her face looks in the morning, before she's awake.

The way her lips curl down.

I think where is that baby?

BODY: Where is that baby?

SOUL: I wonder whether there is a judgement of souls for what they did on earth.

And if there is, I wonder whether I'll go to heaven or to hell.

(*The baby stops crying.*)

BODY: Don't stop crying!

Let me hear you cry!

SOUL: My last thought is about the big red spot on Jupiter, which somebody told me once is actually a huge storm, twice as big as the earth.

BODY: That is one big storm.

SOUL: And then the roof falls on me.

(*The roof collapses.*)

And my body dies.

(*The regular lights come on.*

The WOOER and the WIDOW are home from their date.

The WIDOW carries a plastic bag with leftover tacos.)

WIDOW: The Soul is sleeping.

We have to be quiet.

WOOER: You're the one talking.

(*The WOOER tries to help the WIDOW with her coat but nobody's taken her coat for such a long time, especially since she's at home, so it's weird.*)

SOUL: This isn't a memory.

This is really happening.

I'm in my box.

You didn't see me.

(*The SOUL slips into its box.*)

WIDOW: The Soul is sleeping.

We have to be quiet.

WOOER: You're the one talking.

WIDOW: What?

WOOER: 'We have to be quiet' is a funny thing to say. Don't you think?

I'm just saying that if the point is to be as quiet as possible then we probably shouldn't say anything at all.

I'm just a little nervous. Sorry. I talk when I get nervous.

It's been a long time since I've been in a room with a woman after a very nice dinner.

WIDOW: Me too.

WOOER: When was the last time you were in a room with a woman after a very nice dinner?

WIDOW: What?

WOOER: You said…

WIDOW: No.

WOOER: Oh. I get it now.

WIDOW: A man.

WOOER: I see.

WIDOW: It's been years.

But I guess you knew that.

WOOER: I guess I did.

(*Awkward silence. She takes the tacos and puts them somewhere.*)

Did you know that if you counted twenty-four hours a day
it would take 31,688 years to reach 1 trillion?

WIDOW: No. I didn't know that.

WOOER: I had a cousin who died counting.

WIDOW: How high did he get?

WOOER: A billion-something. Some numbers are bigger than
the imagination.

Did you know that over 2500 left-handed people a year are
killed from using products made for right-handed people?

WIDOW: My husband was left-handed.

WOOER: Fuck. I didn't know that.

WIDOW: I'm just kidding!

WOOER: Did you know that I'm going to kiss you?

(*He pulls her close and kisses her.*

She breaks away.)

I'm sorry.

Did I do something wrong?

WIDOW: It's just fast.

WOOER: I didn't even use my tongue.

WIDOW: I'm sorry.

A kiss with no tongue is fast for me right now.

(*Silence.*)

SOUL: Is it time for my hug?

WIDOW: Not yet.

SOUL: When?

WIDOW: Soon.

WOOER: Listen, I'm going to get going.

WIDOW: Are you sure? I could give it a hug and then we can
keep talking.

WOOER: It's getting late.

WIDOW: Did you catch the game last night?

WOOER: What game?

WIDOW: No game in particular.

WOOER: I had a really nice time.

WIDOW: Do you want a taco for later?

WOOER: I'm good, thanks.

WIDOW: I'd still love to see you again.

> Please call me.

WOOER: Yeah.

> I will. Definitely.
>
> Bye.
>
> (*He slips out very quickly.*)

WIDOW: Bye.

SOUL: I'm proud of you.

WIDOW: But it ended so badly.

SOUL: It's a beginning.

> (*She unlocks the box.*)

WIDOW: It's time for your hug.

SOUL: Oh good. I've been waiting

> (*They hug.*)
>
> Thank you.

WIDOW: You're very very welcome.

> (*After a while she kisses him on the head goodnight.*
>
> *The SOUL goes back down into the box.*
>
> *The WIDOW goes to her closet and takes her nightgown off a hook.*
>
> *A baby cries.*
>
> *Smoke fills the room.*
>
> *The lights fade on the WIDOW.*
>
> *The BODY enters in fireman outfit and axes down the door.*)

BODY: Hold on.

> I'm coming.
>
> (*The SOUL is out of the box.*)

SOUL: I'll say humbly:

BODY: I'm just doing my job.

SOUL: Where is that baby?

BODY: Where is that baby?

SOUL: Is there a judgement of souls for what they did on earth?

> Will I go to heaven or to hell?

(*The baby stops crying.*)

BODY: Don't stop crying!

    Let me hear you cry!

SOUL: My last thought is about the big red spot on Jupiter,

    which is a huge storm, twice as big as the earth.

BODY: That is one big storm.

SOUL: And then the roof falls on me.

    (*The roof collapses.*)

    And my body dies.

    And I was on my way to my final judgement.

    (*The SOUL starts to fly up toward the final judgement.*)

    But my wife caught me.

    (*The WIDOW grabs onto the SOUL.*)

WIDOW: Gotcha.

SOUL: Let me go!

WIDOW: Not quite yet.

SOUL: And I told her:

    This isn't right.

    A soul is not supposed to stay on earth after the body dies.

WIDOW: I'm sorry.

    I need you.

SOUL: I told her that I need to go.

WIDOW: I just need to remember for a little while.

    (*Light fades on the WIDOW.*)

SOUL: It's been more than a little while.

    And I can't forget anything that I ever did in my entire life.

    And I don't know whether what I did was good or bad.

    Whether what I accomplished on earth was of any good to

    anyone.

    (*The baby cries.*

    The BODY enters.)

BODY: Hold on, I'm coming!

    Where is that baby?

    (*The baby stops crying.*)

    Don't stop crying.

(He looks around.)

That is one big storm.

(The roof collapses.

The sun comes up.

The WIDOW is restlessly asleep in bed.)

SOUL: The sun is rising.

It's the morning after my wife's taco date.

This isn't a memory.

This is happening right now.

She didn't sleep very well.

She hasn't slept well since I died. She has dreams that I'm in bed next to her. But she can't remember them.

(The SOUL has a rope made of bedsheets.)

She forgot to lock the lock on my box.

I've been waiting for this day. I made an escape rope out of soiled bed sheets.

(The SOUL ties the bed sheet rope to the box or something solid.)

Before she wakes up, I sneak across the room, careful not to bump into anything.

I listen for the sound of the ocean to find the window.

(The SOUL gropes its way to the window.)

And then I do the worst thing I've ever done.

I leave.

(The SOUL opens the window and throws the bedsheet rope out.

It climbs out.

We hear the sound of the ocean.

The alarm goes off.)

WIDOW: Put the snooze on, honey.

(She wakes up.)

Honey?

Oh. You're dead.

(The WIDOW turns the alarm off herself.

She gets out of bed with a yawn.

Goes to the SOUL's box.)

Wake up, lazy bones.

(*The WIDOW finds out the lock is undone.*

She opens the box.)

Are you playing in my sweaters again?

(*She looks in the closet.*)

Are you playing Marco Polo?

Marco?

(*She goes back into the main room. Sees the bed-sheet rope hanging out the window.*)

Oh no.

(*She pulls the bed-sheet rope all the way in.*

She sticks her head out the window.)

Marco?

(*She brings her head back in.*

She closes the window, slowly.)

Okay.

Okay.

Okay.

(*She goes into the bathroom and turns on the hot water in the sink.*

She takes out a razor blade and closes the bathroom door.)

END OF SCENE ONE

Scene Two

Later that morning.

The WIDOW has bandages on her wrists and blood on her nightgown.
The WOOER looks out the window. He's in his fireman clothes. The red
roses from the night before are dead.

A radio on his shoulder crackles with information that he doesn't
respond to.

WOOER: Did you ever stop to think what effect this would
     have on anyone else?

   There are so many people who care about you in this
   town.

   There's everybody down at the firehouse. And your
   neighbors. People at church.

   I don't know if your parents are still alive, but–
WIDOW: – they're dead.
WOOER: Well. If they were alive they would be sick with grief
   if you left them like this.

   I had a cousin who killed himself once.

   He was an orthodontist who hated teeth and he hung
   himself in his basement with his shoelaces.

   It rocked the foundations of the entire family. You can't
   begin to believe the reverberations that a suicide has.

   (*The radio on his shoulder crackles with information. He doesn't*
   respond.)

   Please, say something.

   What are you thinking about?
WIDOW: I was remembering when I was a little girl and I
   spent the whole summer on my knees in the dirt planting
   marigolds in my grandfather's garden.

   They were his favorite flower.
WOOER: That's a start.

   Talk to me more about marigolds.

WIDOW: They're an annual, part of the daisy family. The
dried petals were once used for coloring butter.

WOOER: Hold the phone.

What's an annual?

WIDOW: An annual is a plant that germinates, flowers, sets
seed and dies within one year.

A perennial is a plant that lives for a few years, some of
which die back to ground level in winter and survive as
underground bulbs.

WOOER: So some plants live their whole lives in one year and
some just pretend they're dead for a while and then keep
on living.

WIDOW: Pretty much.

WOOER: That's amazing.

And your grandfather's favorite flower was the marigold.

WIDOW: And mine.

And my husband's.

Whenever we had a fight he would bring a marigold
wrapped in white paper.

That's what he called me when he was feeling cutesy.

Marigold.

WOOER: But that sounds nothing like your name.

WIDOW: So?

WOOER: It's just nicknames are usually a play on a way a
person's name sounds.

WIDOW: Well I'm sorry!

WOOER: Hey.

My friends used to call me Pope Pius II.

WIDOW: Why did they call you that?

WOOER: I really have no idea.

I think Marigold is a perfectly good nickname for you. Let
me try it out.

Hi, Marigold.

Marigold, would you like to go to the shoe store?

Hey now, Marigold, there's no need for that kind of
language.

WIDOW: Would you have been sad if I died?

WOOER: What?

WIDOW: You talked about people at the firehouse and at
church and my dead parents. But would you have been
sad?

WOOER: I would have been destroyed.

I love you, didn't you already know that?

WIDOW: No. I didn't.

WOOER: I do.

(*And then the top of a ladder appears in the window.*
CAPTAIN O'REILLY appears with the SOUL in tow.)

CAPTAIN O'REILLY: Get in there!

(*He gets the SOUL inside. The SOUL's costume has some holes*
in it. It's been through a couple of bad scrapes.)

WOOER: Where'd you find it?

CAPTAIN O'REILLY: Couple of roofs over.

It was talking to the pigeons.

SOUL: They're very good listeners.

WOOER: Thanks, Captain.

I can take it from here.

WIDOW: You're going straight to bed.

SOUL: But it's still morning.

WIDOW: I don't care what time of day it is.

(*The WIDOW puts the SOUL in the box.*)

SOUL: Can I just say in my defense that you are the one who
left the lock unlocked.

Maybe you unconsciously wanted me to leave.

WOOER: She tried to commit suicide because you left.

SOUL: Really?

WIDOW: Yes, really.

SOUL: I didn't know. How could I?

(*She finally closes the lid.*)

CAPTAIN O'REILLY: May I say something here?

WIDOW: Of course you may.

CAPTAIN O'REILLY: Souls are not really meant to stay on this earth after their time is up. Maybe you should think about letting it go.

WIDOW: I have, thank you.

WOOER: She knows what you're saying, Captain.

CAPTAIN O'REILLY: I am just expressing my opinion, which, if I am not mistaken, I have the right to do in this country. I don't mean to get personal or nothing.

But you know me. You know my wife. My two boys.

You watched them grow up since they were yea high.

WIDOW: I did.

CAPTAIN O'REILLY: And I told my wife, just like I'm sure your husband told you, that if anything, God forbid, ever happens to me, that I would want her to move on and love somebody else.

Because the heart is meant to break. That's what it is made to do. Break, and break, and break again. I shouldn't even say break. I should say sprain. Because your heart cannot break and get paralyzed, like my poor Uncle Jim who fell out of a five-storey window. Your heart is a muscle, and muscles can't break.

I think you're afraid to let yourself love somebody else because that person may in turn die, like your husband died.

And I think that's the real challenge in life, to love in spite of that fact that the object of your love is going to wither and die, just like you yourself are going to wither and die. I know what it's like to curse your heart for having ever loved because if it had never loved you wouldn't feel the repose of loss so distinctly.

But I think you are selling your heart short by pretending it's paralyzed because you're not my Uncle Jim and you didn't fall out of a five-storey window and you can love again.

If you just let yourself.

WIDOW: I'm trying.

CAPTAIN O'REILLY: I know you are, darling.

I know you are.

(*CAPTAIN O'REILLY wraps the WIDOW up in a big hug.*
After a bit he releases her.)

I hope you don't feel that that hug violated your personal boundaries.

WIDOW: Not at all.

It was very nice.

CAPTAIN O'REILLY: We've just had a couple of lawsuits is the only reason I mentioned it.

WOOER: She's not gonna sue, Captain.

WIDOW: I'll sign a waiver.

CAPTAIN O'REILLY: No need for that.

It's just some people don't like getting hugged.

That's the lesson I learned.

But I'm glad you don't mind it.

WIDOW: Me too.

WOOER: I'll take it from here, Captain.

CAPTAIN O'REILLY: Okey dokey.

I'll be in the truck.

You taking the ladder or the stairs?

WOOER: I'll take the stairs.

CAPTAIN O'REILLY: Suit yourself.

(*CAPTAIN O'REILLY climbs down the ladder.*)

Coming down boys. Who needs a hug?

(*The ladder disappears.*)

WOOER: Can I take you out on another date?

WIDOW: If you want to.

WOOER: I do.

WIDOW: Then yes.

WOOER: I have to work doubles the rest of this week.

What about Friday?

WIDOW: Friday's fine by me.

WOOER: I can get us tickets to the opera. My cousin is an usher and can get us real good seats.

How does that sound?

WIDOW: That sounds great.

WOOER: Your husband wasn't into the opera or anything, was he?

WIDOW: No. He sang in the shower, but never opera. Mostly Roberta Flack.

WOOER: Because I love the Ernestos, but I want to take you out to something real classy.

(*Information crackles on the shoulder radio.*

The WOOER talks into the radio curtly.)

Ten-four. I'll give you a hug in a minute.

(*He puts the radio back.*)

I'll pick you up at seven.

WIDOW: I'll be here.

WOOER: (*Quietly, so the SOUL doesn't hear.*) Do you mind if I kiss you?

WIDOW: (*Quietly, too.*) You don't have to ask.

(*The WOOER kisses her.*

Fire engine honks from outside. The WOOER kisses her one more time.)

WOOER: Goodbye.

WIDOW: Goodbye.

(*The WOOER goes out the door.*

The WIDOW sits on the SOUL's box sadly.

A baby cries.)

I hear my baby crying.

(*The lights fade, except for on the WIDOW.*)

The one I miscarried.

(*She looks for the baby.*)

I look for it.

Where are you, Sam?

If it was a girl I was going to name it Samantha and call her Sam, because I love girls who have boy's names. And if it was a boy I was going to name him Samuel, because my favorite author is Mark Twain, and his real name was Samuel Clemens.

So either way I look for Sam.

Sam!

Where are you, darling?

I can't find you.

Keep crying. Momma's gonna find you.

(*The baby stops crying.*)

But I can never find it.

(*The BODY enters.*)

BODY: It's okay.

WIDOW: This is after the miscarriage. He brought me a marigold wrapped in white paper.

He said 'It's okay. We'll have another one. We'll have ten more.'

(*The BODY has a marigold wrapped in white paper.*)

BODY: It's okay.

We'll have another one.

We'll have ten more.

WIDOW: But we never did. Something happened with my eggs and my tubes. They said I couldn't have any children.

(*It's bedtime.*)

BODY: Time for bed.

WIDOW: I'm not tired.

BODY: You have to sleep.

WIDOW: No I don't. I'll stay up forever.

BODY: That's irrational.

WIDOW: Then I'm irrational.

BODY: I'm going to sleep.

WIDOW: Go to sleep.

He falls asleep so quickly, and talks in his sleep.

BODY: (*Mumbling in his sleep.*) Turn me over. Yeah, that's just right.

WIDOW: I barely ever sleep anymore.

And since my husband died I stopped dreaming.

I have to remember my old dreams.

I used to dream that I could fly.

But I never actually flew.

I was always teaching other people to fly.

(*The WOOER appears. Flying.*)

There you go.

Now just think up.

(*The WOOER crashes into something.*)

Up!

Up!

WOOER: I am thinking up!

(*The WOOER flies higher.*)

WIDOW: There you go.

Now you're getting the hang of it.

WOOER: I think I'm getting the hang of it!

(*Pause.*)

What do I do now?

WIDOW: I don't know. Keep flying.

WOOER: Where should I go?

WIDOW: Wherever you want.

WOOER: I don't know where I want to go.

WIDOW: You could try Boca Raton. I hear it's beautiful this
time of year.

WOOER: Okay. I'll fly to Boca. Thanks.

WIDOW: Don't mention it.

(*The WOOER flies off.*)

Now when I sleep it's just black.

Or if I do dream I don't remember it anymore.

(*The lights change to the morning.*

The WIDOW lies in bed reading a book. The BODY gets ready
for work. He turns on the shower, and brushes his teeth.)

This is the morning he died.

BODY: I don't know what you want me to say.

WIDOW: I don't want you to say anything.

BODY: I said I was sorry.

WIDOW: We had a fight the night before.

We were never good at fighting.

(*To the BODY.*) I heard you.

BODY: I apologized. You're supposed to say it's okay.

WIDOW: It's okay.

BODY: You have to mean it.

WIDOW: But I don't.

BODY: Fuck this. I have to get ready for work.

(*The BODY goes into the shower.*)

WIDOW: Fuck this. I have to get ready for work.

Those are the last words he ever said to me.

(*The BODY sings 'Killing me Softly' in the shower.*)

And in the shower he sang 'Killing me Softly'.

He wasn't much of a singer.

That morning I put Kleenex in my ears because I was so mad.

This is what I wish I had said to him:

(*She goes into the bathroom and opens the shower curtain.*)

Through the ups and downs, this is a richer life than I ever imagined for myself. You know how perennial flowers pretend to die every year? I just wanted to tell you that I am a flower and you are the sun and your absence is winter and without you I'm dead.

(*Pause.*)

BODY: Thanks.

(*She closes the shower curtain.*)

WIDOW: But I didn't say any of that.

Instead I put Kleenex in my ears.

(*She puts Kleenex in her ears.*)

And I can't ever forget those last words.

(*The lights change.*

Some old rock and roll rises. Different than the first high school dance.)

This is the first time we met.

It was at a dance in high school.

We were high school sweethearts. Was he really that handsome?

BODY: You bet I was.

(*The BODY appears ready for a high school dance.*)

WIDOW: These are the first words he ever said to me:

BODY: Hey, you wanna dance?

WIDOW: It began so simply.

I said no.

'No, thank you.'

But he kept at it.

BODY: Why not?

WIDOW: Does there need to be a reason?

BODY: No. I'm just wondering. I happen to be a very curious person.

WIDOW: I don't feel like dancing.

BODY: You don't have a gimp leg or anything?

WIDOW: I'm perfectly healthy. If you must know I used to be a ballerina.

BODY: So you don't mind dancing.

WIDOW: I love it.

BODY: So it's me you don't like.

WIDOW: That's right.

BODY: Did you ever notice me? I mean, 'cause I noticed you.

In the library. You're always reading.

Why do you read so much?

WIDOW: Because I like to pretend I'm somebody else.

BODY: That's kinda sad.

WIDOW: I don't think it's sad.

I think it indicates that I have an active imagination.

BODY: Why don't we imagine we're in a book and I'm somebody you're in love with and you really want to dance with me?

WIDOW: That was twice as charming as it needed to be.

I said fine:

Fine.

And we danced.

(*They dance.*)

Unfortunately, he wasn't a very good dancer.

Owww.

BODY: Sorry.

WIDOW: He put his arms in the small of my back.

(*He pulled me tight and I could feel his erection in my hip.*)

BODY: Ummmm, those are my car keys.

WIDOW: Sure they are.

(*The BODY whispers into her ear.*

She giggles.

They go out back to the car.)

And I let him take me to the back seat of his car.

And I let him take my dress up over my waist.

And I let him I let him I let him.

(*They have sex, doggy-style.*)

He came within twenty seconds.

(*He comes.*)

BODY: Sorry.

WIDOW: It's okay.

BODY: I'll do better next time.

WIDOW: I got pregnant.

And we got married.

He joined the fire department to support the baby instead of going to college.

But I lost the baby.

(*The baby cries. The BODY appears with a marigold wrapped in white paper.*)

BODY: It's okay.

We'll have another one.

We'll have ten more.

(*The BODY leaves.*

The WIDOW searches for the baby.)

WIDOW: Where are you, Sam?

Keep crying.

I'm gonna find you.

Keep crying.

GRANDFATHER: Stop all that crying.

WIDOW: That's my grandfather.

I'm eight years old.

It's the summer. I'm in his garden.

GRANDFATHER: Stop all that crying and let me show you a thing or two.

(*The baby stops crying.*

The WIDOW puts on a sunhat.

Gets down in the dirt with her GRANDFATHER.)

Plants have a life cycle. Flowers grow and die the same time every year and that makes them easier to love than people.

WIDOW: What about Grandma?

GRANDFATHER: What about her?

WIDOW: Did she die according to a schedule?

GRANDFATHER: No.

One night she went to sleep and simply didn't feel like waking up.

WIDOW: Did you cry when Grandma died?

GRANDFATHER: Yes, I did.

WIDOW: If I died would you cry?

GRANDFATHER: Of course I would.

Would you cry if I died?

WIDOW: I would cry a whole river.

GRANDFATHER: Then it's settled.

WIDOW: Grandpa?

GRANDFATHER: Yes?

WIDOW: Do you know when you're going to die?

Because I have school in three weeks and then I turn nine and I have my birthday party to go to.

GRANDFATHER: No, I don't know when I'm going to die.

WIDOW: Would you tell me if you did?

GRANDFATHER: Of course I would.

WIDOW: But you know when this marigold is going to die.

GRANDFATHER: I can't say for certain. It might get stepped on by a little girl I know.

WIDOW: That was one time!

GRANDFATHER: Or the weather might get to it. There might be an early frost.

WIDOW: But you know when it's supposed to die.

GRANDFATHER: I do. In the fall.

WIDOW: Wouldn't it be nice if people died in the fall, too? Just like flowers.

GRANDFATHER: Yes, it would be nice.

Come on, let's go inside and get us a glass of lemonade.

WIDOW: What if I want two glasses of lemonade?

GRANDFATHER: Then two you shall have.

(*He begins to go.*)

WIDOW: (*No longer a little girl.*) That's what I always said to him.

What if I want two glasses of lemonade?

And he always said the same thing.

GRANDFATHER: Then two you shall have.

WIDOW: He died two years later but I couldn't cry.

I didn't really understand he was dead until they told me I couldn't go to his house for the summer.

That I had to stay home.

(*The GRANDFATHER is gone.*

The BODY is back to the morning he died.

To the fight.)

BODY: I don't know what you want me to say.

WIDOW: I don't want you to say anything.

BODY: I said I was sorry.

WIDOW: I heard you.

BODY: I apologized. You're supposed to say it's okay.

WIDOW: It's okay.

BODY: You have to mean it.

WIDOW: I do mean it.

I'm so sorry that we got into this fight to begin with.

I love you so much.

Please give me a kiss and tell me you love me.

BODY: Fine.

But I'm still mad.

(*The BODY kisses her. She holds onto his neck. Doesn't let him go.*)

What's gotten into you?

WIDOW: Nothing.

BODY: Seriously.

I gotta get to work.

(*He kisses her on the head.*)

WIDOW: Tell me you love me.

BODY: I do.

WIDOW: You what?

BODY: I love you.

WIDOW: Call in sick.

BODY: But I'm not sick.

WIDOW: We could just lie in bed all day and eat figs.

BODY: Figs?

WIDOW: It sounded like what lovers would eat in bed.

BODY: We're not lovers, we're married.

WIDOW: Please.

BODY: I'm sorry.

(*He goes into the shower. Sings 'Killing me Softly'.*
She listens.)

WIDOW: He was such a terrible singer.

Even though I miss him I'll never miss his singing.

(*She goes into the bathroom and undoes the shower curtain.*)

We had happy times, didn't we?

BODY: Of course we did.

WIDOW: You could always make me laugh.

BODY: I tried to.

WIDOW: I wish I could remember the happy times.

BODY: I'm sorry.

We're not in control of what we remember and what we forget.

(*He closes the shower curtain and sings 'Killing Me Softly'. The WOOER appears in fireman clothes.*)

WOOER: Something happened.

There was a baby trapped in a house. Your husband wouldn't leave.

He's a hero.

(*The WOOER leaves.*)

WIDOW: And I went down to the house where my husband died.

And I saw his soul leave his body and try to get to judgement or wherever souls go after they leave the earth.

(*The SOUL begins to fly toward judgement.*)

But I caught it before it could go.

(*She catches the SOUL.*)

Gotcha.

SOUL: Let me go!

WIDOW: And I put it in this box.

(*The WIDOW puts the SOUL in the box.*)

Get in there.

SOUL: This isn't right.

A soul isn't supposed to stay on earth after the body dies.

WIDOW: I'm sorry.

I need you.

SOUL: And I need to go.

WIDOW: I just need to remember for a little while.

And then you can go.

(*The SOUL cries.*)

And a little while became a little longer.

It's been two years since you died.

It was fall, like it is now, and the leaves had already fallen. Not that much has changed. I still drink gin and tonic. I still believe happiness never really lasts, I still watch the 'Macy's Thanksgiving Day Parade', and I still love you.

I've tried my best not to. I've tried so hard to forget.

SOUL: I know you've tried.

WIDOW: Every day I wake up and think maybe today is the day I won't remember.

And it never is. Every day is the same.

I wear the same black dress. I walk around in the same circles. One of these days I'm going to wear a hole in the floor.

SOUL: Today is different.

WIDOW: Is it?

Is it really different?

SOUL: You're going on your first date since I died.

WIDOW: A date that turns out badly and doesn't help me forget.

SOUL: You forget for a few minutes here and there.

WIDOW: But then I remember the rest of the time.

SOUL: It's a beginning.

(*The WOOER appears with boxes. He's going through the closet, taking out clothes.*)

WOOER: What about this sport coat?

WIDOW: (*To the SOUL.*) I have to go. More memories.

SOUL: I understand.

WOOER: What about this sport coat?

WIDOW: Keep it.

WOOER: What about these shoes?

WIDOW: Keep them.

WOOER: What about his uniform?

WIDOW: No way, not that.

WOOER: You've got to get rid of something.

WIDOW: I need those shoes.

WOOER: What are you going to do with these shoes?

WIDOW: Whatever I want.

WOOER: I'm getting rid of them.

WIDOW: I said no.

WOOER: You've got to get rid of something.

WIDOW: Not the shoes.

WOOER: Fine. The sport coat.

WIDOW: I need it.

WOOER: You don't need a sport coat.

WIDOW: Yes I do.

WOOER: What's the point of going through his clothes if you're not going to get rid of anything?

WIDOW: Here.

(*The WIDOW gives the WOOER a pair of socks.*)

I don't need those.

WOOER: A pair of socks?

WIDOW: He never wore them. Not once.

WOOER: So everything he ever wore you're keeping.

WIDOW: Maybe.

WOOER: I don't know why you asked me to help you.

I took off work.

WIDOW: I thought I was ready.

I guess I'm not.

WOOER: This is just a waste of my time.

WIDOW: I'm sorry.

(*The WOOER goes.*)

SOUL: That didn't go so well.

WIDOW: I couldn't bear to part with anything.

(*She picks up the sport coat. Smells it.*)

It still smells like you.

Even after all this time.

(*The BODY appears in a tie.*)

BODY: Well, let's see if it still fits.

(*The WIDOW puts the sport coat on the BODY.*)

WIDOW: Perfect.

BODY: I look okay?

WIDOW: You look so handsome.

BODY: Are you ready to go?

WIDOW: I am.

BODY: I hope you're ready to shake that ass 'cause I'm in the mood to boogie.

WIDOW: Let's go.

(*Music rises. They're at the fireman's ball. Maybe there's a mirror ball.*)

SOUL: Welcome to the Downtown Holiday Inn for this year's Fireman's Ball.

(*They dance. Not a slow dance. A fast one. The BODY is going for it. The WOOER appears. They all dance together. The WOOER tries to do the electric slide. He's not so good. Everybody laughs. Everybody's happy. After a while the song is over.*)

WIDOW: No. I want to remember this some more.

BODY: Sorry.

(*He goes with the WOOER. The SOUL leaves too. She is alone. She breathes. She doesn't quite know what to do.*

The WOOER appears, dressed like he was in the beginning.)

WOOER: I had no idea you had a miscarriage.

WIDOW: It's not your fault.

How could you have known?

(*The BODY appears back at the fight.*)

BODY: I don't know what you want me to say.

WIDOW: I don't want you to say anything.

WOOER: I know, but I'm sorry anyway.

WIDOW: Thanks.

That's sweet of you to say.

(*The baby cries. Only the WIDOW hears it.*)

SOUL: So make big talk.

WIDOW: What's big talk?

BODY: I said I was sorry.

WIDOW: I heard you.

WOOER: You look really beautiful.

Did I already tell you that?

WIDOW: You did.

SOUL: Ask him if he thinks each person's soul is judged for the things they do on earth.

(*She begins to look around for the baby. More and more frantically.*)

WOOER: Oh.

Sorry.

Sometimes when I get nervous I repeat myself.

WIDOW: You don't have to apologize.

Where are you Sam?

BODY: I apologized. You're supposed to say it's okay.

WIDOW: It's okay.

SOUL: Fine.

Talk about the weather.

Talk about whatever you like.

WOOER: I'm not very good at small talk.

WIDOW: Come on, darling.

Keep crying.

Momma's gonna find you.

WOOER: I can't stand it when people talk about sports or gossip or the weather.

WIDOW: Keep crying!

BODY: You have to mean it.

SOUL: I don't know. I hope not.

WOOER: I just wanted to tell you that tonight means a lot to me.

BODY: Fuck this. I have to get ready for work.

WIDOW: Momma's gonna find you.

(*The WOOER leaves like he's leaving with the WIDOW on their date.*

The BODY goes into the shower.

The SOUL goes into its box.

The WIDOW stays behind looking for the crying baby. Which stops crying.)

Don't stop crying, baby.

I want to be a momma to you.

Don't you know that?

If I could just find you I could be your momma.

(*The BODY brings a marigold wrapped in white paper.*)

BODY: It's okay.

We'll have another one.

We'll have ten more.

WIDOW: But we don't.

Something happened with my eggs and my tubes.

BODY: We could adopt.

WIDOW: We never did that either.

And then one day you died.

BODY: I'm sorry.

Everything that's alive has to die.

(*The BODY goes.*)

WIDOW: And I try to forget.

I have to forget.

(*The WOOER appears dressed up for their date for the opera in a rented tuxedo. He has little opera glasses. New, sort of tacky alligator shoes. He knocks on the door with a tappity tap tap. He has marigolds.*)

Who is it?

WOOER: It's your handsome date.

WIDOW: This isn't a memory.

It will be soon but right now it's happening.

WOOER: I hope you're ready for some 'Rigoletto'.

WIDOW: It's one week later.

I'm going to the opera.

I have to get changed.

(*Calling.*) Just a minute!

I'll be dressed in a jiff.

WOOER: Take your time!

(*She changes into her green dress and checks her hair.*
The WOOER sings 'La donna è mobile' ('Woman is fickle')
from 'Rigoletto'.
And then she's ready.)

WIDOW: I take a deep breath.

(*She takes a deep breath.*)

I open the door and he kisses me hello.

He says I look stunning.

(*The WOOER kisses her hello on the cheek.*)

WOOER: You look stunning.

WIDOW: I compliment his new shoes even though I don't mean it.

WOOER: Alligator.

Wrestled it myself.

WIDOW: And he says this time he brought marigolds.

WOOER: This time I brought marigolds.

WIDOW: I say: 'They're beautiful.'

And they are.

(*She sets them down.*)

And he offers me his arm.

(*He offers his arm.*)

And I take it.

(*She takes it.*)

He asks, 'Shall we go?'

WOOER: Shall we go?

WIDOW: And I say, we shall.

We shall.

And we go to the opera, and I have a much better time than I expected.

(*They leave. She holds his arm tight.*)

END OF SCENE TWO

Scene Three

The WOOER and the WIDOW barge in the door, making out.
Tongue and everything. There's some petting. Some might describe it as heavy.

WOOER: Shhhh.

    We gotta be quiet.

WIDOW: You're the one talking.

WOOER: I'm going to use my tongue.

WIDOW: Do your worst.

    (*They make out more.*
    He sticks his hand under her dress.
    She takes it out.)

    Not here. The Soul is sleeping.

WOOER: Where can we go?

WIDOW: There's the closet or the bathroom.

WOOER: The bathroom. I like tile.

WIDOW: The bathroom it is.

    (*He kisses her.*)

    Get in there.

    (*She spanks him.*)

WOOER: You coming?

WIDOW: Let me slip into something a little more comfortable.

WOOER: That is fucking awesome.

    Nobody has ever said that to me in my whole life.

    (*He goes into the bathroom.*
    Shuts the door.
    The WIDOW takes off her dress. She's in just her bra and panties.
    She considers her different more comfortable options.
    One's too demure. One's too much.
    The bathroom door opens a crack.
    The WOOER is singing 'The Stripper'. He doesn't have to sing it, it just sort of comes on.
    A hand comes out of the bathroom holding the ugly alligator shoes.
    They drop to the ground.

And then the coat. The necktie.
The shirt.
The belt, swung around like a lasso.
The pants.
The underwear.
She picks the too much comfortable outfit.
Slips it on.
She's about to go to the bathroom when the SOUL starts crying in the box.
If you need to cover a costume change, use the following:
WOOER: This is a really nice bathroom.

 I should know, my cousin works on bathrooms.

 The tile work is so intricate.

 Is this your perfume? Ooo la la. French.

 I've never been to France. But I used to wear a beret.

 And speak with a French accent.

 I demanded that everyone call me Gerard.

 I don't remember why.

 Hey, are you almost finished slipping into something more comfortable?

 WIDOW: Almost…)

SOUL: Is it time for my hug?

WIDOW: No. It's not.

SOUL: I'm sorry to break up your party.

WIDOW: It's okay.

 Can you just be quiet for like twenty minutes?

SOUL: I'll try.

WOOER: (*In the bathroom.*) Come on Marigold, don't be shy.

WIDOW: Five minutes.

 Three.

 Please.

 I almost forgot you.

 This is what you want.

SOUL: I'm scared of being judged for what I did on earth.

WIDOW: What you did on earth was good.

You were a hero.

SOUL: I was just doing my job.

If I thought that roof was going to collapse I would have left that baby.

WIDOW: But you didn't.

SOUL: I did so many terrible things.

WIDOW: They couldn't have been that bad.

WOOER: What's taking so long?

SOUL: I was a terrible lover.

WIDOW: That's true.

But you can't go to hell for that.

WOOER: I'm freezing my ass off. Seriously.

SOUL: When I was a kid I shot a BB through a window and an old lady lost her eye and a month later she died.

WIDOW: Little boys get into mischief.

SOUL: I wanted to get divorced after your miscarriage.

WIDOW: I know.

SOUL: You knew that?

WIDOW: And I would have let you go but I couldn't be alone.

SOUL: How did you know?

WIDOW: I don't know. I just knew.

SOUL: And you don't think that makes me bad.

WIDOW: It doesn't make you great, but I don't think you're going to go to hell.

SOUL: No?

WIDOW: No.

SOUL: Thank you.

Because I've been so worried.

WOOER: Seriously. My nuts are up in my stomach.

SOUL: Oh, come on man!

WIDOW: Shhhh.

Can we talk about this later?

SOUL: Of course.

Get in there and have some sex.

Are you nervous?

WIDOW: No.

I'm excited.

SOUL: I'm so happy for you.

Can I have a hug? Even if it's not time yet.

A hug to give you away.

WIDOW: Just a quick one.

(*She unlocks the box and the two of them hug.*)

SOUL: Why don't you let me go?

WIDOW: I can't do everything in one night.

SOUL: Sure you can.

You're ready.

WIDOW: I might be ready to make love but that doesn't mean
I'm ready to live without you.

SOUL: Make a clean break.

That's the best way.

WIDOW: I never thought so.

I always took my Band-Aids off slowly and got into the
ocean inch by inch.

I don't like clean breaks.

SOUL: I would feel better if I wasn't here.

It's going to be a little weird knowing you're in the
bathroom having sex with another man.

(*The WOOER comes out in a towel.*

He's jacked.)

WOOER: What's the problem?

SOUL: There's no problem.

WIDOW: I'm coming.

SOUL: She's going to forget me!

You're going to have sex.

Everything's going to work out.

(*The SOUL cries.*)

WOOER: Why is it crying?

SOUL: I'm not crying.

I'm laughing.

WIDOW: Let's go in the bathroom, baby.

WOOER: It's not laughing.

WIDOW: You're right.

(*The SOUL cries.*)

WOOER: I can't concentrate on my sexual technique if I know
your dead husband's soul is out here crying.

SOUL: I'll stop crying.

I promise.

WIDOW: It was a mistake to try this here.

We'll try again next week and go to your place.

WOOER: We can't go to my place.

I live with my mom.

WIDOW: You do?

SOUL: Really?

WOOER: What? Does that make me less appealing or
something?

WIDOW: No.

I just didn't know that.

It's just new information to me.

(*The SOUL laughs, in spite of itself.*)

WOOER: Are you laughing at me?

SOUL: No.

I'm crying.

(*The SOUL pretends to cry.*)

WOOER: So what's it gonna be?

Is it the Soul or me?

WIDOW: I need to take this slow.

WOOER: You should choose me. I'm here, I'm in this room,
I'm alive.

SOUL: He's got a good point.

WIDOW: If I have to choose right now I choose the Soul.

SOUL: Fuck.

WOOER: I understand.

(*He collects his clothes from the bathroom and is about to go.*)

WIDOW: Can I take a rain check?

WOOER: I don't know.

This hot and cold thing is really getting to me.

I've waited so long for someone to love. And I think you're the someone I've been waiting to love, but the problem is I don't think you're ready to be loved, you know what I mean?

WIDOW: I do.

I'm trying real hard.

WOOER: I know you are.

WIDOW: I'm sorry if I hurt you.

WOOER: You did. Hurt me.

But it's okay.

I don't blame you.

WIDOW: Can I have a kiss before you go?

WOOER: No.

I'm sorry. You can't have a kiss.

I think it would hurt too much.

(*The WOOER's about to go.*)

WIDOW: Sorry. But that was my husband's towel.

WOOER: Oh.

I'll mail it to you.

(*He exits.*)

SOUL: Is he gone?

WIDOW: Yes. He's gone.

SOUL: Did he take my towel?

WIDOW: Yes he took your towel.

SOUL: Damn.

So it's just you and me again.

WIDOW: Yes. It's just you and me.

SOUL: I'm guessing it's not time for my hug.

WIDOW: Not even close.

SOUL: Do you want to have a conversation? Small talk, big talk, either one.

WIDOW: No thanks.

SOUL: Marco Polo?

WIDOW: No.

SOUL: We could play in your sweaters?

WIDOW: I'm not in the playing mood.

SOUL: You're never going to let me go, are you?

WIDOW: I don't know.

    Maybe not.

SOUL: I'm going to try to escape now.

WIDOW: I figured.

SOUL: You could let me go.

WIDOW: I could.

SOUL: But you won't.

WIDOW: No.

SOUL: Are you ready?

WIDOW: As ready as I'll ever be.

SOUL: Here I go.

    (*The SOUL tries to make it to the window. He does some shake*
    and bake moves, like a running back in football.
    The WIDOW stops the SOUL.
    The SOUL bites her.
    She hits it in the head.
    They go offstage.
    We hear crashes, yells, screams of pain.
    It's a Battle Royale. The BODY bounds on.
    And then we hear crying.
    It's the BODY. He comes out from the shadows with his axe.
    He talks slowly, because he's not so good with words.)

BODY: Hold on, I'm coming!! This isn't the right scene.

    I don't know what you want me to say. Wrong.

    We'll have another one. We'll have ten more.

    Hello?

    I'm alone.

    This play hurts me.

    Somebody told me about a man named Syphillis who had
    to roll a boulder up a hill all day every day and when he
    got to the top the boulder fell to the bottom and he had to
    start all over again.

I am Syphillis.

This play is my boulder. I push it scene by scene, and I think maybe I can take a rest.

But then I have to have the fight with my wife.

And then the baby I can never find starts crying and I have to chop down the door.

The smoke burns my eyes and my heart breaks, because I never find it.

Sometimes I imagine what I would say to the baby, if I could ever find it.

(*He picks up a pillow, maybe from the bed.*)

I will pretend this pillow is the baby in question.

(*He holds it like a baby.*)

Do not worry, baby.

I have saved you.

You are safe here in my arms.

And I imagine I would take this baby from the fire and raise it as my own.

And he or she would grow up and we would play catch.

(*A CHILD enters.*)

CHILD: You wanna play catch, Dad?

BODY: I would love to play catch.

What should we play catch with?

I do not have a ball.

CHILD: We could use that lamp.

BODY: Why don't we use this pillow?

CHILD: Okay, Dad.

(*The BODY tosses the CHILD the pillow.*
It drops the pillow.)

Sorry.

BODY: It's not your fault.

CHILD: Whose fault is it, Dad?

BODY: It is your fault.

But I don't blame you.

CHILD: Thanks, Dad.

(*It picks up the pillow and throws it back to the BODY.*
Awkwardly.)

BODY: Good throw.

CHILD: Stop lying.

(*The BODY throws the pillow back.*
The CHILD drops it again.)

It's a good thing we didn't play catch with the lamp.

BODY: You're right.

CHILD: I'm sorry you died trying to find me.

BODY: I am too.

CHILD: I really wanted you to find me.

BODY: Me too.

It's all I wanted.

CHILD: Do you think you would have liked me?

I mean, assuming that I didn't die in the fire and you didn't
die in the fire and you raised me as your own.

BODY: I think I would have loved you.

CHILD: Maybe next time they remember the fire you'll find
me?

BODY: I don't think there is going to be a next time.

CHILD: So this is our last hurrah.

BODY: I'm afraid so.

CHILD: Do you mind if I hug you?

BODY: Why would I mind?

CHILD: I heard some people don't like it, that's all.

BODY: I would love a hug from you.

(*The CHILD hugs the BODY.*
The CHILD is done.
The BODY keeps hugging.)

CHILD: You're hurting me.

(*The BODY hugs harder.*)

Dad.

I can't breathe.

BODY: It's better this way.

This way you won't have any memories.

CHILD: Please.

BODY: Shhhhh.

> (*The CHILD is dead.*)
>
> I am going to dispose of the body of my imaginary child. I will return in a minute.
>
> (*The BODY drags it offstage.*
>
> *We hear the fight between the SOUL and the WIDOW. It's crazy.*
>
> *The BODY comes back onstage.*
>
> *The WIDOW drags the SOUL in.*
>
> *She's bleeding. Her hair is all fucked up.*
>
> *The SOUL's costume is ripped to shreds.*
>
> *She takes a pill. She washes it down with some gin.*
>
> *The BODY enters.*)

WIDOW: What were you doing?

BODY: I just disposed of the body of our imaginary child.

WIDOW: Ours.

BODY: Yours and mine. It was fairly devastating.

> You two had quite a skirmish.

WIDOW: Gives new meaning to wrestling with a soul, huh?

BODY: That's not funny.

WIDOW: It wants to go so badly.

BODY: So do I. This play hurts us both so much. It hurts you too.

> (*The SOUL wakes up.*)

SOUL: Did I win?

WIDOW: No.

> You got your ass kicked.

SOUL: Fuck me.

WIDOW: Let's keep going. Let's do a happy memory of a simple morning.

> (*The WIDOW gets into bed.*)

BODY: I am really not in the mood. I just killed a child.

SOUL: And I just got my ass kicked.

BODY: But you do not have to talk.

SOUL: But I have to watch.

WIDOW: I'm waiting.

SOUL: She's waiting.

BODY: Is there any alternative?

SOUL: I don't think so.

BODY: Fine. But do not expect me to enjoy it.

(*The BODY gets in next to her.*

The alarm goes off.)

WIDOW: Snooze it, will you, honey?

BODY: I've got to get up.

WIDOW: Five more minutes.

BODY: I'll be late.

(*He tickles her.*)

WIDOW: Don't tickle.

BODY: Get up, lazy bones.

WIDOW: I'll get up when you get up.

BODY: I'm up.

WIDOW: Your eyes are still closed.

BODY: But I'm like totally awake.

WIDOW: You get out of bed first and then I will.

BODY: It's your turn.

WIDOW: It was my turn yesterday.

BODY: We'll both go together.

WIDOW: On the count of three.

BODY / WIDOW: One, two, three.

WIDOW: You didn't move.

BODY: You didn't either.

WIDOW: Okay for real this time.

BODY / WIDOW: One, two, three.

(*They both hop out of bed.*)

WIDOW: I'm tired.

(*She yawns.*)

BODY: You were talking in your sleep.

WIDOW: What did I say?

BODY: You said, 'Turn me over. Yeah, that's just right.'

WIDOW: No, I didn't.

BODY: I swear to God you did.

(*They go about their morning routines.*)

WIDOW: You missed a spot.

BODY: Where?

WIDOW: Under your chin.

BODY: What would I do without you?

WIDOW: You'd shave badly.

This was a mistake.

SOUL: That's not your line.

Try again.

WIDOW: I'm going to the store.

Do you want prunes or plums?

BODY: Prunes. My shit is like bricks.

WIDOW: Crunchy or creamy peanut butter?

BODY: Crunchy.

No.

Creamy.

No.

Crunchy.

Fuck.

WIDOW: I'll get both.

BODY: Good idea.

WIDOW: I can't go on.

SOUL: You can try.

WIDOW: You're dead. You don't want to be here.

SOUL: I haven't wanted to be here for two years.

BODY: Neither have I.

WIDOW: I'm sorry.

BODY: Now she's sorry.

WIDOW: This was a mistake. You were right.

SOUL: I have to say I told you so.

WIDOW: It's been two years since you died.

I still believe happiness never really lasts, I still watch the 'Macy's Thanksgiving Day Parade', and I still love you.
But now, I'm ready to forget.

BODY: Everything that begins has to end.

SOUL: And this is how this ends. I say goodbye and you say…

WIDOW: Goodbye.

SOUL: And the Body says…

BODY: I hope for nothing. I fear for nothing. I am free.

SOUL: Nope.

BODY: Between grief or nothing I will take grief?

SOUL: Try again.

BODY: Goodbye?

SOUL: Good job.

> (*The SOUL takes off.*)
>
> And I fly. At first I'm scared of what's to come.
>
> I fly over the whole earth.
>
> And even though I don't have eyes I see everyone.
>
> If they're awake I see their lives, and if they're asleep I see their dreams.
>
> And what I see makes me laugh.
>
> (*The SOUL laughs.*)
>
> I laugh not because it's exactly ha ha funny.
>
> Maybe I laugh because I'm scared.
>
> But maybe because there's nothing else to do.
>
> (*The SOUL laughs.*)
>
> And I leave the earth and fly past Jupiter and whoever judges souls judges that I get to go to heaven. So I fly to heaven, where there are no memories or pain or sickness or sadness or hunger or disease or hatred or fear.
>
> And all I do is laugh.
>
> (*The SOUL disappears above the ceiling, laughing.*)

BODY: Well, that's my cue.

> (*He opens a door in the floor of the stage.*)

WIDOW: Are you going to be okay down there?

BODY: Sure.

> I get to lie in the dark all day every day and all night every night.
>
> I get to rest.

(The WIDOW hugs the BODY.)

Thank you for the hug.

I needed it.

WIDOW: You're welcome.

BODY: And I go under the earth where I rest, the only
exertion I make is when I push up a couple of marigolds.
As I go I sing, 'Killing Me Softly', just for old time's sake.
*(The BODY goes down through the door, singing 'Killing Me
Softly'. It closes the door behind him.)*

WIDOW: And then I am finally alone.

(She is alone.)

And I breathe.

(She breathes.)

And my heart beats.

(Her heart beats.)

Out of reflex. Out of no will of my own.

Because that's what hearts do.

They beat and they break.

And then I sleep.

(She lies down to sleep.)

And I dream that I'm flying.

(She flies.)

I fly above the neighborhoods and places I've lived.

I fly above all the people I have ever known.

I fly past the cemetery where my husband is buried.

And then I fly home.

To my empty bed.

(She flies gracefully into bed.)

I used to only sleep on my side but now I sleep right in the
middle.

(The sun rises.)

And then the sun rises and it's another day.

*(The back wall disappears.
There is a sea of orange marigolds and perfect white light.)*

I wake up and I feel reborn.

(The WOOER enters.

He knocks on the door five times so we know it's him.)

WOOER: And I enter and go to the door and bang on it and say:

'I'm sorry about last night.'

WIDOW: And I don't answer.

(The WOOER bangs on the door.)

WOOER: And I say:

'Just give me another chance.

My cousin's an event planner and can get us into a really great after party.'

WIDOW: And I don't answer.

WOOER: Hey.

That was your cue.

I say, 'My cousin's an event planner and can get us into a really great after party.'

And then you open the door.

(The WIDOW packs a bag.)

WIDOW: And I pack a bag.

I get ready to go.

WOOER: And then you open the door.

And we kiss.

And I say I'm sorry.

And you say you're sorry, although you don't know what you're sorry about.

And we accept the changing nature of life, and the inevitable loss that accompanies change, and we love each other in spite of the fact that we're both going to die, most likely without cause or warning.

WOOER: Hey.

What are you doing?

Are you committing suicide again?

WIDOW: No.

I found a way out.

There's a sea of orange marigolds.

WOOER: Hold the phone. You found what?

WIDOW: There is a sea of orange marigolds.

They were here the whole time but I never knew it.

WOOER: What am I supposed to do?

WIDOW: Remember.

WOOER: But we didn't spend enough time together.

I don't have enough memories.

WIDOW: They'll have to do.

WOOER: That's not fair.

WIDOW: I'm sorry.

But I found my way out.

WOOER: Fine! But I'm going to keep going.

(*The WOOER exits.*

The WIDOW looks at us.

She goes to the edge of the room.

She puts a foot into the marigolds.)

WIDOW: Goodbye.

(*The WIDOW walks out the back of the set.*

She walks into the marigolds.

The WOOER appears at the door like he did in the beginning,

looking nervous holding flowers. He wears a suit and tie.)

WOOER: I knock on the door.

(*He knocks on the door.*)

And you say, 'I'll just be a minute! I just got out of the shower!'

And I say, 'Take your time!'

And I spray breath freshener in my mouth.

(*He sprays breath freshener in his mouth.*)

I check my hair.

(*He checks his hair.*)

I check my armpits. To make sure they don't smell.

(*He checks his armpits to make sure they don't smell.*)

And I think, 'This is it.

I've been waiting my whole life for this. Waiting for somebody I can love.

After tonight I won't have to wait anymore.'
After tonight my life can finally begin.'
(*The WIDOW disappears in the flowers.*
And the perfect light gets brighter and brighter.
Until it fills the whole stage and covers the audience too.)

THE END